F|O|C|U|S
ON PRONUNCIATION 1

LINDA LANE

American Language Program
Columbia University

Longman

Focus on Pronunciation 1

Pearson Education, 10 Bank Street, White Plains, NY 10606

Executive editor: Laura Le Dréan
Associate acquisitions editor: Dena Daniel
Development manager: Paula H. Van Ells
Marketing manager: Joe Chapple
Production editor: Andréa Basora
Production manager: Ray Keating
Senior manufacturing buyer: Nancy Flaggman
Cover and text design: Pat Wosczyk
Cover photo: © Dimitri Veritsiotis/Digital Vision, Ltd.
Project management and text composition: Elm Street Publishing Services, Inc.
Text font: 11.5/13 Minion
Pronunciation diagrams: Tracey Cataldo
Text art: Jill Wood

Library of Congress Cataloging-in-Publication Data

Lane, Linda (Linda L.)
      Focus on pronunciation. 1 / Linda Lane.
         p. cm.
      ISBN 0-13-097873-6—ISBN 0-13-097877-9—ISBN 0-13-097879-5
      1. English language—Pronunciation—Problems, exercises, etc. 2.
English language—Textbooks for foreign speakers. I. Title: FOP1. II.
Title.
PE1137.L22 2005
428.3'4—dc22   2004008145

ISBN: 0-13-097873-6

LONGMAN ON THE **WEB**

Longman.com offers online resources for teachers
and students. Access our Companion Websites, our
online catalog, and our local offices around the world.

Visit us at **longman.com**.

Printed in the United States of America
2 3 4 5 6 7 8 9—VH—07 06 05

CONTENTS

ABOUT *FOCUS ON PRONUNCIATION 1*

Focus on Pronunciation 1 is a comprehensive course that helps beginning students speak English more clearly and accurately. The course covers important topics from all aspects of pronunciation—sounds, stress, rhythm, and intonation.

ORGANIZATION OF *FOCUS ON PRONUNCIATION 1*

Focus on Pronunciation 1 is divided into three parts: Vowels, Consonants, and Stress, Rhythm, and Intonation. Each part begins with an overview unit. The overview unit presents important topics included in that part. The units following the overview deal in depth with specific pronunciation points.

The Self-Study section at the back of the book provides additional practice with pronunciation points. Students can use this material on their own outside of class, or it can be used as an additional source of classroom practice.

UNIT ORGANIZATION

The units following the overviews typically have the following organization:

INTRODUCTION
The Introduction presents and explains the pronunciation point. It may show how sounds are made or present other useful information on the pronunciation point. Its purpose is to make students aware of the pronunciation point.

FOCUSED PRACTICE
This section contains classroom practice activities. The activities are designed to ensure student involvement through games, interactive tasks, and listening/speaking activities dealing with high-interest topics.

- Students first work on controlled activities that allow them to develop skill and proficiency with the particular point.
- They then practice the point in more communicative activities. When students are engaged in the communicative activities, they should be encouraged to keep in mind these global features of clear speaking:
  - Speak Slowly
  - Speak Loudly Enough
  - Pay Attention to the Ends of Words
  - Use Your Voice to Speak Expressively

ON YOUR OWN
The homework section usually includes one or more controlled exercises and a freer speaking task.

CDs

The Classroom CDs for *Focus on Pronunciation 1* include all the recorded activities for the course. In addition, there are Student CDs that include the On Your Own and Self-Study exercises. Students can record the activities from On Your Own on a cassette, which they can turn in to the teacher for comment. Alternatively, students could record sound files on the computer to send in e-mails to the teacher.

KEY TO ICONS

🎧 —material recorded on the full audio program

🎧 —material recorded on the Student CDs

🔲 —pair activity

🔲 —group activity

▣ —material for students to record and give to the teacher

PLANNING A SYLLABUS

The units in *Focus on Pronunciation 1* can be used in any order. In my own teaching, I like to "skip around"—for example, teaching the overview unit for Vowels, then a specific vowel unit, then the overview for Stress, Rhythm, and Intonation, then a specific unit dealing with rhythm, and so on. Teachers who adopt this approach could also cover all the overview units at the beginning of the course and then skip around within the sections. The units can also be taught in order, first covering vowels, then consonants, and so on.

REFERENCES

The following research influenced the content and method of this book.

Avery, Peter and S. Ehrlich. *Teaching American English Pronunciation.* Oxford: Oxford University Press, 1992.

Celce-Murcia, Marianne, D.M. Brinton and J. M. Goodwin. *Teaching Pronunciation: A Reference for Teachers of English to Speakers of Other Languages.* Cambridge: Cambridge University Press, 1996.

Dauer, Rebecca. *Accurate English.* Prentice Hall Regents, 1993.

ACKNOWLEDGMENTS

I am indebted to a number of people whose support, patience, and good humor made this book possible. I am grateful for the help and suggestions of my editors at Pearson: Eleanor Barnes, Ginny Blanford, Laura Le Dréan, Karen Davy, Paula Van Ells, Dena Daniel, Andréa Basora, and Kathleen Silloway. I would also like to give special thanks to Michele McMenamin, who wrote the Self-Study exercises for *Focus on Pronunciation 1*.

I am grateful for the insightful comments and suggestions of the reviewers: Dr. John Milbury-Steen, Temple University, Philadelphia, PA; Michele McMenamin, Rutgers University, Piscataway, NJ; Gwendolyn Kane, Rutgers University, Piscataway, NJ; William Crawford, Georgetown University, Washington, D.C.; Linda Wells, University of Washington, Seattle, WA; Tara Narcross, Columbus State Community College, Columbus, OH; Robert Baldwin, UCLA, Los Angeles, CA; Mary Di Stefano Diaz, Broward Community College, Davie, FL; Barbara Smith-Palinkas, University of South Florida, Tampa, FL; Susan Jamieson, Bellevue Community College, Bellevue, WA; Andrea Toth, City College of San Francisco, San Francisco, CA; Fernando Barboza, ICPNA, Lima, Peru; Adrianne P. Ochoa, Georgia State University, Atlanta, GA; Greg Jewell, Drexel University, Philadelphia, PA; Cindy Chang, University of Washington, Seattle, WA; Emily Rosales, Université du Québec à Montréal/École de Langues, Montréal, QC, Canada.

I would also like to express my thanks to my colleagues at the American Language Program at Columbia University, who used these materials in their own classes, for their advice and feedback.

For the encouragement and patience of my family, Mile, Martha, Sonia, and Luke, and of my dear friend Mary Jerome, I am deeply grateful.

Finally, I want to thank my students—for teaching me how they learn pronunciation, for wanting to improve their pronunciation, and for showing me how to help them.

Linda Lane

ABOUT THE AUTHOR

Linda Lane is a faculty member in the American Language Program of Columbia University. She is coordinator of Columbia's TESOL Certificate Program, where she also teaches Applied Phonetics and Pronunciation Teaching and Introduction to Second Language Acquisition. She received her Ed.D. in Applied Linguistics from Teachers College, Columbia University, and her M.A. in Linguistics from Yale University.

PART
1

VOWELS

UNIT **1** Vowel overview

INTRODUCTION

🎧 There are 14 vowel sounds in English. Listen to these words.

1. s<u>ee</u> [iy]
2. b<u>i</u>g [ɪ]
3. w<u>ai</u>t [ey]
4. w<u>e</u>t [ɛ]
5. h<u>a</u>t [æ]
6. c<u>u</u>p [ə]
7. st<u>o</u>p [ɑ]

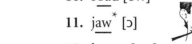

8. f<u>oo</u>d [uw]
9. b<u>oo</u>k [ʊ]
10. r<u>oa</u>d [ow]
11. j<u>aw</u>[*] [ɔ]
12. h<u>ou</u>se [aw]
13. <u>eye</u> [ay]
14. b<u>oy</u> [oy]

FOCUSED PRACTICE

| **1** | **LISTEN AND PRACTICE:** *Four vowels end in a* [y] *sound.* |

🎧 Listen.

[ay]	[oy]	[ey]	[iy]
<u>eye</u>	b<u>oy</u>	pl<u>ay</u>	t<u>ea</u>

🎧 A. Listen to these words and repeat them.

1. t<u>oy</u>s
2. d<u>ay</u>
3. fl<u>y</u>

4. wh<u>y</u>
5. t<u>a</u>ble
6. tr<u>ee</u>

7. b<u>ee</u>
8. pl<u>ea</u>se
9. <u>oi</u>l

10. n<u>oi</u>se
11. m<u>y</u>
12. f<u>a</u>ce

B. Write each word from Part A in the correct column.

[ay] **eye**	[oy] **boy**	[ey] **play**	[iy] **tea**
_____	*toys*	_____	_____
_____	_____	_____	_____
_____	_____	_____	_____

---

[*] Many Americans say *j<u>aw</u>* with the vowel in *st<u>o</u>p*.

C. Listen to these sentences and repeat them. Use [y] to join the vowel to the next word.

1. The boy is sick.
2. Please say it again.
3. Today is Saturday.
4. Why are you laughing?
5. Try it again.
6. Let's see a movie.

2 LISTEN AND PRACTICE: *Three vowels end in a* [w] *sound.*

Listen.

[aw] cow   [ow] go   [uw] shoe

A. Listen to these words and repeat them.

1. owl
2. know
3. how
4. pool
5. brown
6. student
7. two
8. boat
9. toes

B. Write each word from Part A in the correct column.

[aw] **cow**	[ow] **go**	[uw] **shoe**
owl		

C. Listen to these sentences and repeat them. Use [w] to join the vowel to the next word.

1. Do it now.
2. It's too easy.
3. Go away.
4. Show it to me.
5. How is your friend?
6. The cow is sick.

3 LISTEN AND PRACTICE: *Key words* [æ], [ɑ], [ɪ], [ɛ], [ə], *and* [ʊ]

A. Listen to these words and repeat them. Then match them to the word or words with the same vowel.

Key words 1

1. bag [æ]
2. father [ɑ]

 a. laugh
 b. job
 c. hat
 d. glasses

Key words 2

1. big [ɪ]
2. bed [ɛ]

 a. head
 b. pig
 c. building
 d. sit

Key words 3

1. cup [ə]
2. book [ʊ]

 a. sun
 b. push
 c. love
 d. cook

4 BINGO: *Vowels*

A. Listen to these words.

1. a. wait
   b. wet

2. a. seat
   b. sit

3. a. Luke
   b. look

4. a. head
   b. had

5. a. leave
   b. live

6. a. hat
   b. hot

7. a. cup
   b. cop

8. a. will
   b. well

∩ B. Listen again. Which word from Part A do you hear? Circle *a* or *b*.

∩ C. Listen to the words on the Bingo card and repeat them.

1. head	5. hot	9. will	13. seat
2. cup	6. wait	10. Luke	14. hat
3. look	7. wet	11. had	15. leave
4. well	8. sit	12. cop	16. live

∩ D. Now play Bingo. Use the card in Part C. Listen carefully and put an *X* over the words you hear. When you have four *X*s in a row, say "Bingo!"

5 CURRENCY

Currency means "money." In the United States, the currency is the dollar. Different countries have different names for their currencies.

∩ A. Listen to the names of the currencies in column A. Match the underlined vowel sounds from each word in column A with the same underlined vowel sound in column B.

A	B
_____ 1. ruble	a. wet [ɛ]
_____ 2. peso	b. stop [ɑ]
_____ 3. dollar	c. shoe [uw]
_____ 4. yen	d. go [ow]
_____ 5. krona	e. play [ey]

B. Work with a partner. The countries in the box use one of the currencies in Part A. Write the name of the country in the blank.

| Sweden | Canada | Japan | Russia | Mexico |

C. Do you know the names of other currencies? Write them on the board with the country name. What currency is used in your country?

UNIT 2 [iy] <u>ea</u>t and [ɪ] <u>i</u>t

INTRODUCTION

Look at the pictures. They show you how to say the sounds of [iy] and [ɪ].

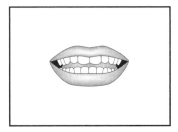

<u>ea</u>t [iy]

Spread your lips.
End the vowel with [y].

<u>i</u>t [ɪ]

Relax your lips.
Lower your tongue a little.

Spellings for [iy]	Spellings for [ɪ]
Common	**Common**
n<u>ee</u>d, s<u>ee</u>, f<u>ee</u>t	s<u>i</u>t, m<u>i</u>nute, r<u>i</u>ch **$$$**
bel<u>ie</u>ve, p<u>ie</u>ce	
<u>ea</u>st, r<u>ea</u>d	
pol<u>i</u>ce, sk<u>i</u>	
Other	**Other**
rec<u>ei</u>ve	b<u>ui</u>ld
p<u>eo</u>ple	b<u>u</u>sy, b<u>u</u>siness
k<u>ey</u>	g<u>i</u>ve, l<u>i</u>ve

FOCUSED PRACTICE

1 LISTEN AND PRACTICE: *Words with* [iy]

A. Listen to these words and repeat them.

1. see	5. green	9. leave	13. sheep
2. be	6. people	10. these	14. week
3. me	7. feel	11. machine	15. eat
4. tree	8. police	12. please	16. teach

B. Choose four words from Part A and write them on the lines.

Your words:

_____   _____   _____   _____

C. Work with a partner. Read your words to your partner. Your partner will write what you say. Then listen to your partner's words. Write them on the lines.

Partner's words:

_____   _____   _____   _____

2 LISTEN AND PRACTICE: *Words with* [ɪ]

A. Listen to these words and repeat them.

1. visit	5. thin	9. this	13. hit
2. milk	6. fish	10. big	14. sit
3. minute	7. swim	11. sister	15. sick
4. with	8. quick	12. listen	16. window

B. Choose four words from Part A and write them on the lines.

Your words:

_____   _____   _____   _____

C. Work with a partner. Read your words to your partner. Your partner will write what you say. Then listen to your partner's words. Write them on the lines.

Partner's words:

_____ _____ _____ _____

3 | BINGO: *Words with* [iy] *and* [ɪ]

A. Listen to these words.

1. **a.** meat
   b. mitt

2. **a.** sheep
   b. ship

3. **a.** heat
   b. hit

4. **a.** seat
   b. sit

5. **a.** eat
   b. it

6. **a.** green
   b. grin

7. **a.** heel
   b. hill

8. **a.** reach
   b. rich

B. Listen again. Which word from Part A do you hear? Circle *a* or *b*.

C. Listen to the words on the Bingo card and repeat them.

1. heel	5. reach	9. it	13. eat
2. mitt	6. sheep	10. green	14. meat
3. ship	7. grin	11. rich	15. heat
4. hit	8. seat	12. hill	16. sit

D. Now play Bingo. Use the card in Part C. Listen carefully and put an *X* over the words you hear. When you have four *X*s in a row , say "Bingo!"

LISTEN FOR DIFFERENCES: [iy] *vs.* [ɪ]

A. Listen to these sentences and repeat them.

1.

     a. That's a high hill.   **b.** That's a high heel.

2.

     a. The meat is on the mitt.   **b.** The mitt is on the meat.

3.

     a. The ship is on the sheep.   **b.** The sheep is on the ship.

B. Listen again. Which sentence from Part A do you hear? Circle *a* or *b*.

C. Work with a partner. Take turns reading a sentence from Part A. Your partner will point to the sentence you said.

5 JOIN WORDS TOGETHER: [iy] + a/an

A. Listen to these sentences and repeat them. Use [y] to join *be* to *a* or *an*.

1. I'd like to be ^{y}a doctor.

2. I want to be ^{y}a singer.

3. I'd like to be ^{y}a mechanic.

4. I want to be ^{y}a writer.

5. I want to be ^{y}an engineer.

6. I'd like to be ^{y}a politician.

B. Choose two sentences from Part A and write them on the lines.

Your sentences:

_____

_____

C. Work with a partner. Read your sentences to your partner. Your partner will write what you say. Then listen to your partner's sentences. Write them on the lines.

Partner's sentences:

_____

_____

6 INTERVIEWS: *Do you have a job?*

A. Listen to the job names. Circle the words with the [iy] sound. Underline the words with the [ɪ] sound.

1. a singer

2. a teacher

3. a musician

4. a businessperson

5. a comedian

6. an electrician

7. a police officer

8. a politician

9. a TV cameraperson

B. Interview three classmates and write their answers in the chart on the following page. You can use these models.

Student 1: Do you have a job now?

Student 2: *Yes.*

Student 1: What do you do?

Student 2: *I'm a secretary.*

Student 1: Do you like your job?

Student 2: *Yes. The people at work are very nice.*

OR

Student 1: Do you have a job now?

Student 2: *Not a paying job—I'm a student.*

Student 1: What kind of job would you like?

Student 2: *I'd like to be singer.*

Student 1: Why?

Student 2: *I love to sing, and I want to be famous.*

	Name _____	Name _____	Name _____
1. Do you have a job now?			
2. If yes:			
a. What do you do?			
b. Do you like your job? Why?			
3. If no:			
a. What kind of job would you like?			
b. Why?			

C. Report the information from your chart to the class.

🎧 **First listen to:**
- the sentences in Exercises 4 and 5.

📼 **Now record them.**

How are your [iy] and [ɪ] sounds?

Self-Study: See page 149.

UNIT 3 [æ] b<u>a</u>d and [ɛ] b<u>e</u>d

INTRODUCTION

Look at the pictures. They show you how to say the sounds of [æ] and [ɛ].

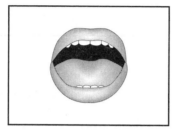

[æ]

Open your mouth.
Spread your lips.
Push your tongue down
and to the front.

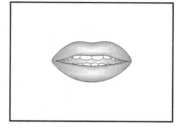

[ɛ]

Your mouth is almost closed.
Spread your lips.

Spellings for [æ]	Spellings for [ɛ]

Common
    b<u>a</u>d, h<u>a</u>t, pl<u>a</u>stic
Other
    l<u>au</u>gh
	Common
	    b<u>e</u>d, g<u>e</u>t, n<u>e</u>ver
	Other
	    br<u>ea</u>kfast, w<u>ea</u>ther
	    ag<u>ai</u>n, s<u>ai</u>d, ag<u>ai</u>nst
	    fri<u>e</u>nd
	    <u>a</u>ny, m<u>a</u>ny

FOCUSED PRACTICE

A. Listen to these words and repeat them.

1. bad	5. ask	9. family	13. dance
2. have	6. angry	10. stand	14. after
3. that	7. hat	11. cat	15. black
4. answer	8. thanks	12. fat	16. happy

B. Choose four words from Part A and write them on the lines.

Your words:

_____ _____ _____ _____

C. Work with a partner. Read your words to your partner. Your partner will write what you say. Then listen to your partner's words. Write them on the lines.

Partner's words:

_____ _____ _____ _____

A. Listen to these words and repeat them.

1. bed	5. men	9. friend	13. breakfast
2. left	6. heavy	10. then	14. pen
3. west	7. dress	11. never	15. yesterday
4. said	8. dead	12. yellow	16. leg

B. Choose four words from Part A and write them on the lines.

Your words:

_____ _____ _____ _____

C. Work with a partner. Read your words to your partner. Your partner will write what you say. Then listen to your partner's words. Write them on the lines.

Partner's words:

_____ _____ _____ _____

BINGO: *Words with* [æ] *and* [ɛ]

A. Listen to these words.

1. **a.** Dad
   b. dead

2. **a.** had
   b. head

3. **a.** sad
   b. said

4. **a.** laughed
   b. left

5. **a.** man
   b. men

6. **a.** Annie
   b. any

7. **a.** Brad
   b. bread

8. **a.** bad
   b. bed

B. Listen again. Which word from Part A do you hear? Circle *a* or *b*.

C. Listen to the words on the Bingo card and repeat them.

1. Dad	5. man	9. head	13. bed
2. left	6. bad	10. any	14. Brad
3. said	7. bread	11. men	15. sad
4. had	8. dead	12. laughed	16. Annie

D. Now play Bingo. Use the card in Part C. Listen carefully and put an *X* over the words you hear. When you have four *X*s in a row, say "Bingo!"

LISTEN FOR DIFFERENCES: [æ] *vs.* [ɛ]

A. Listen to the sentences in column A.

	A	**B**
1.	Do you like bread?	**a.** Yes, he's very nice.
	Do you like Brad?	**b.** Yes, with butter.

2. Spell *head*.   a. H-A-D.

Spell *had*.   b. H-E-A-D.

3. He took my pan.   a. Now you can't write.

He took my pen.   b. Now you can't cook.

4. My father just left.   a. Did you say something funny?

My father just laughed.   b. When is he coming back?

B. Match the sentences in columns A and B in Part A to make dialogues.

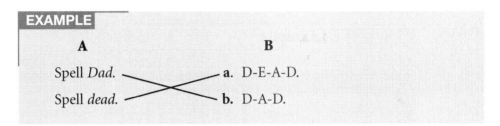

EXAMPLE

A	**B**
Spell *Dad*.	a. D-E-A-D.
Spell *dead*.	b. D-A-D.

C. Work with a partner. Take turns reading a sentence from column A in Part A and answering with the correct response from column B.

5   WORD GROUPS: *Breakfast foods*

A. Listen to the items on the breakfast menu. Do you know what the words mean?

Breakfast Menu

Main Dishes

Scr<u>a</u>mbled <u>e</u>ggs	$1.50
Fried <u>e</u>ggs	$1.50
P<u>a</u>ncakes with syrup	$3.00
Waffles with b<u>e</u>rries	$3.00
Cereal with milk	$2.00

Side Dishes

H<u>a</u>sh-brown potatoes	$1.00
Br<u>ea</u>d or toast	$1.00
Muffin (corn, br<u>a</u>n)	$1.00
Bagel with cream cheese	$1.50
Bacon	$1.00
H<u>a</u>m	$1.00

Beverages

Orange juice	$1.00
<u>A</u>pple juice	$1.00
Coffee	$ .75
Tea	$ .75
Milk	$1.00
Hot chocolate	$1.50

B. Look at the words with underlined letters in Part A. Write each word in the correct column.

[æ]	[ɛ]
scrambled	*breakfast*
_____	_____
_____	_____
_____	_____
_____	_____

6 DIALOGUE

A. Read this dialogue. Make sure you understand all the words. The underlined sounds are [æ] or [ɛ] vowels.

Dan: Alice, do you eat breakfast?

Alice: No, I'm always on a diet.

Sonia: So am I—but I have to eat breakfast.
When I get up, I'm starving!

Dan: Do you eat a big breakfast? You know, like ham and eggs?

Sonia: No, just cereal. And coffee. I have to have coffee.

Alice: Me too. I do have coffee—but just black. And nothing else.

Dan: They say you'll eat less later if you have breakfast.

Sonia: And you have more energy.

Alice: I don't! I feel slow and heavy all day if I eat breakfast.

B. Listen to the dialogue in Part A.

C. In groups of three, practice reading the dialogue in Part A.

7 INTERVIEW: *What do you have for breakfast?*

Work with a partner. Talk about your breakfast habits. Use the dialogue in Exercise 6 and the menu in Exercise 5 for ideas.

🎧 **First listen to:**

- the words in Exercises 1, 2, and 3.

📼 **Now record them.**

How are your [æ] and [ɛ] sounds?

Listen to the dialogues in Exercise 4. Record the dialogues.

Self-Study: See pages 149–150.

[æ] BAD AND [ɛ] BED   17

INTRODUCTION

Look at the pictures. They show you how to say the sounds of [ɑ] and [ə].

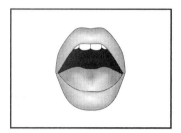

[ɑ]
Open your mouth.

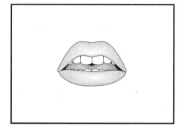

[ə]
Your mouth is almost closed.

Spellings for [ɑ]	Spellings for [ə]

Common
  n<u>o</u>t, d<u>o</u>ctor
  f<u>a</u>ther
	Common
	  b<u>u</u>t, h<u>u</u>ngry
	
	Other
	  m<u>o</u>ney, d<u>o</u>ne, c<u>o</u>lor
	  en<u>ou</u>gh
	  bl<u>oo</u>d

FOCUSED PRACTICE

I **LISTEN AND PRACTICE:** *Words with* [ɑ]

A. Listen to these words and repeat them.

1. st<u>o</u>p
2. w<u>a</u>tch
3. <u>o</u>ften
4. cl<u>o</u>ck
5. j<u>o</u>b
6. c<u>o</u>p
7. n<u>o</u>t
8. f<u>a</u>ther
9. b<u>o</u>ttle
10. h<u>o</u>t
11. pr<u>o</u>blem
12. d<u>o</u>ctor
13. l<u>o</u>t
14. b<u>o</u>x
15. s<u>o</u>ccer
16. w<u>a</u>nt

B. Choose four words from Part A and write them on the lines.

Your words:

_____   _____   _____   _____

C. Work with a partner. Read your words to your partner. Your partner will write what you say. Then listen to your partner's words. Write them on the lines.

Partner's words:

_____   _____   _____   _____

2 LISTEN AND PRACTICE: *Words with* [ə]

A. Listen to these words and repeat them.

1. cup	5. brother	9. come	13. month
2. money	6. young	10. sun	14. summer
3. number	7. country	11. mother	15. love
4. bus	8. some	12. under	16. color

B. Choose four words from Part A and write them on the lines.

Your words:

_____   _____   _____   _____

C. Work with a partner. Read your words to your partner. Your partner will write what you say. Then listen to your partner's words. Write them on the lines.

Partner's words:

_____   _____   _____   _____

3 LISTEN FOR DIFFERENCES: [ɑ] vs. [ə]

A. Listen to these words and repeat them.

1. **a.** shot   **b.** shut

2. **a.** boss*   **b.** bus

3. **a.** collar*   **b.** color

4. **a.** dock   **b.** duck

5. **a.** cot   **b.** cut

B. Listen again. Which word from Part A do you hear? Circle *a* or *b*.

4 LISTEN AND PRACTICE: *Sentences with* [ɑ] *and* [ə]

A. Listen to these sentences and repeat them.

1. Chickens go "cluck-cluck," and clocks go "tick-tock."
2. What color is your collar?
3. My boss takes the bus.
4. People who win lotteries are lucky.
5. The cot is not comfortable.
6. How much money is enough?
7. The ducks are swimming near the docks.

---

* Some people pronounce these words with [ɔ].

B. Look at the words with underlined letters in Part A. Write each word in the correct column.

[ɑ]	[ə]
clocks	_____
_____	_____
_____	_____
_____	_____
_____	_____
_____	_____
_____	_____
_____	_____
_____	_____

C. Work with a partner. Practice saying the sentences in Part A.

5 LISTENING FOR DIFFERENCES: [ɑ] vs. [ə]

A. Listen to the sentences in column A.

A	B
1. How do you spell *once*?	**a.** W-A-N-T-S.
How do you spell *wants*?	**b.** O-N-C-E.
2. Let's go swimming near the duck.	**a.** No, boats tie up there.
Let's go swimming near the dock.	**b.** No, we'll scare it.
3. That's a new cop.	**a.** It's very pretty.
That's a new cup.	**b.** He looks very young.
4. I shut the door.	**a.** You have a gun?
I shot the door.	**b.** Please open it.

B. Match the sentences in columns A and B in Part A to make dialogues.

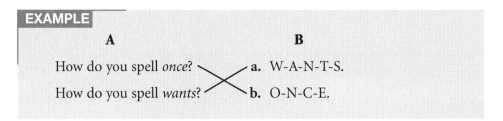

EXAMPLE

A	B
How do you spell *once*?	**a.** W-A-N-T-S.
How do you spell *wants*?	**b.** O-N-C-E.

C. Work with a partner. Take turns reading a sentence from column A in Part A and answering with the correct response from column B.

ON YOUR OWN

🎧 **First listen to:**

- the words in Exercises 1 and 2.
- the sentences in Exercise 4.

▭▭ **Now record them.**

How are your [ɑ] and [ə] sounds?

Self-Study: See page 150.

INTRODUCTION

Look at the pictures. They show you how to say the sounds [ə], [æ], and [ɑ].

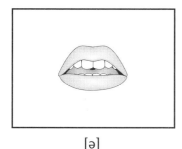

[ə]
The mouth is almost closed.

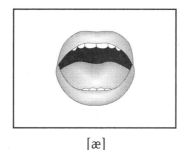

[æ]
The mouth is open.
The lips are spread.

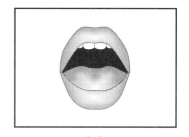

[ɑ]
The mouth is open.
The lips are not spread.

FOCUSED PRACTICE

I	**LISTEN AND PRACTICE:** *Words with* [ə], [æ], *and* [ɑ]

🎧 A. Listen to these words and repeat them.

	[ə]	[æ]	[ɑ]
1.	**a.** cup	**b.** cap	**c.** cop
2.	**a.** done	**b.** Dan	**c.** Don
3.	**a.** nut	**b.** Nat	**c.** not
4.	**a.** run	**b.** ran	**c.** Ron
5.	**a.** bug	**b.** bag	**c.** bog

B. Listen again. Which word from Part A do you hear? Circle *a, b,* or *c.*

C. Choose one row from Part A and write the words on the lines.

Your words:

_____   _____   _____

D. Work with a partner. Read your words to your partner. Your partner will write what you say. Then listen to your partner's words. Write them on the lines.

Partner's words:

_____   _____   _____

2   WORD GROUPS: *Family*

A. Make sure you understand these family words.

1. mother	4. husband	7. father	10. mom	13. son
2. aunt*	5. younger	8. cousin	11. uncle	14. dad
3. daughter	6. grandmother	9. brother	12. grandfather	15. family

B. Listen to the words in Part A and repeat them.

C. Look at the words in Part A. Write each word in the correct column.

[ə]	[æ]	[ɑ]
mother	_____	_____
_____	_____	_____
_____	_____	_____
_____	_____	_____
_____	_____	_____
_____	_____	_____
_____	_____	_____

_____

* Some people pronounce *aunt* and *daughter* with [ɔ], a vowel similar to [ɑ].

D. Complete Sam's family tree with words from Part A.

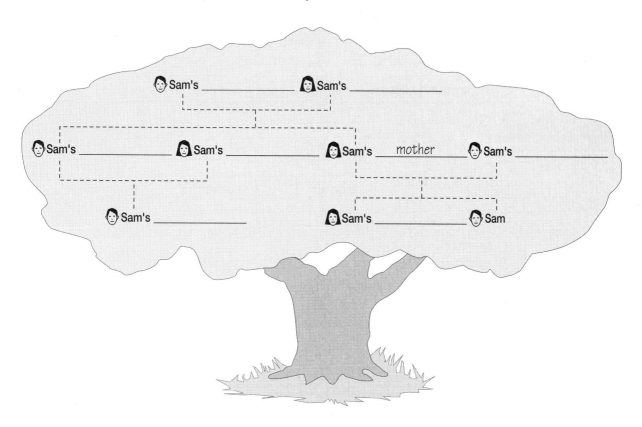

Sam's _____   Sam's _____

Sam's _____   Sam's _____   Sam's _mother_   Sam's _____

Sam's _____   Sam's _____   Sam

| 3 | **DIALOGUES** |

A. Read these dialogues. Make sure you understand all the words.

1. **A:** Do you have any brothers or sisters?
    B: No. I'm an only child.

2. **A:** How many brothers and sisters do you have?
    B: I have two brothers.

3. **A:** Are you the oldest?
    B: No, I'm a middle child. My sister is the oldest.

4. **A:** Do you have any children?
    B: Yes. I have a son and a daughter.

5. **A:** Are you married?
    B: No, but I'm engaged.

B. Listen to the dialogues in Part A.

C. Work with a partner. Practice the dialogues in Part A.

4   INTERVIEWS: *Tell me about your family.*

A. Ask three classmates about their families. Use the dialogues in Exercise 3 for ideas. Write the answers in the chart below.

	Name _____	**Name** _____	**Name** _____
Brothers and sisters?			
Married/ Single?			
Children?			

B. Report your information to the class. Who has the largest family? How many of your classmates are married? How many have children?

ON YOUR OWN

First listen to:
- the words in Exercises 1 and 2.

Now record them.

Then record a one-minute description of your family.

Self-Study: See page 151.

UNIT 6 — Vowels + *r*: [ɑr] c<u>ar</u>, [or] f<u>our</u>, and [ər] b<u>ir</u>d

INTRODUCTION

Look at the pictures. They show you how to say the sound [r] and the sounds [ɑr], [or], and [ər].

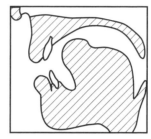

Turn the front of your tongue up and back to make [r].

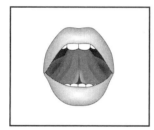  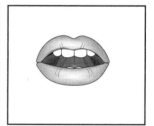

car [ɑr]	**four** [or]	**first** [ər]
Your mouth is open. Your tongue turns up and back.	Your lips are round. Your tongue turns up and back.	Your mouth is almost closed. Your tongue turns up and back.

Spellings for [ɑr]	**Spellings for** [or]	**Spellings for** [ər]
Common 　c<u>ar</u>, h<u>ar</u>d	Common 　f<u>or</u>, m<u>or</u>e 　fl<u>oor</u>, d<u>oor</u>	Common 　h<u>er</u>, w<u>er</u>e 　t<u>ur</u>n, b<u>ur</u>n 　f<u>ir</u>st, b<u>ir</u>d
Other 　h<u>ear</u>t 　g<u>uar</u>d	Other 　f<u>our</u> 　w<u>ar</u>, w<u>ar</u>m	Other 　h<u>ear</u>d, <u>ear</u>th 　w<u>or</u>k, w<u>or</u>d

FOCUSED PRACTICE

1 LISTEN AND PRACTICE: *Words with* [ɑr]

🎧 A. Listen to these words and repeat them. Open your mouth. Turn your tongue up and back.

1. garden	5. apartment	9. arm
2. car	6. dark	10. park
3. hard	7. start	11. star
4. smart	8. heart	12. party

B. Choose four words from Part A and write them on the lines.

Your words:

_____   _____   _____   _____

C. Work with a partner. Read your words to your partner. Your partner will write what you say. Then listen to your partner's words. Write them on the lines.

Partner's words:

_____   _____   _____   _____

2 LISTEN AND PRACTICE: *Words with* [or]

🎧 A. Listen to these words and repeat them. Round your lips. Turn your tongue up and back.

1. four	5. shore	9. north
2. more	6. short	10. war
3. store	7. story	11. warm
4. floor	8. door	12. sports

B. Choose four words from Part A and write them on the lines.

Your words:

_____   _____   _____   _____

C. Work with a partner. Read your words to your partner. Your partner will write what you say. Then listen to your partner's words. Write them on the lines.

Partner's words:

_____ _____ _____ _____

3 LISTEN AND PRACTICE: *Words with* [ər]

A. Listen to these words and repeat them. Keep your mouth almost closed and small inside. Turn your tongue up and back.

1. bird	5. sir	9. burn
2. first	6. shirt	10. turn
3. circle ◯	7. birthday	11. work
4. dirty	8. thirsty	12. learn

B. Choose four words from Part A and write them on the lines.

Your words:

_____ _____ _____ _____

C. Work with a partner. Read your words to your partner. Your partner will write what you say. Then listen to your partner's words. Write them on the lines.

Partner's words:

_____ _____ _____ _____

4 SAME OR DIFFERENT?: [ɑr] *vs.* [or] *vs.* [ər]

A. Listen to the word pairs. If the underlined sounds are the same, write *S*. If they are different, write *D*.

1. were, work _S_	6. third, turn ___
2. third, more ___	7. heart, heard ___
3. word, wore ___	8. war, car ___
4. start, hard ___	9. circle, her ___
5. learn, bird ___	10. door, store ___

B. Choose two pairs from Part A that are the same and two pairs that are different. Write them on the lines. Then work with a partner. Take turns reading a pair of words aloud and writing the words you hear.

	Same	**Different**
Your words:		
	—————— , ——————	—————— , ——————
	—————— , ——————	—————— , ——————
Partner's words:		
	—————— , ——————	—————— , ——————
	—————— , ——————	—————— , ——————

---

5 LISTEN AND PRACTICE: *Sentences with* [ɑr], [or], *and* [ər]

A. Listen to these sentences and repeat them.

1. I heard the class is hard.
2. Her birthday is March 1st (first).
3. I need to learn more words.
4. He parked his car in front of the store.
5. I hurt my arm at the party.
6. The door is always locked on Thursday morning.

B. Look at the words with the underlined letters in Part A. Write each word in the correct column.

[ɑr]	[or]	[ər]
——————	——————	*heard*
——————	——————	——————
——————	——————	——————
——————	——————	——————
——————	——————	——————
——————	——————	——————

C. Practice the sentences with a partner.

6 GAME: *Vowels + r*

Play this game in two teams—Team 1 and Team 2.

Team 1: Ask the questions on page 181 to the players on Team 2.

Team 2: Answer the questions with a word that has the [ɑr], [or], or [ər] vowel. Then ask Team 1 the questions on page 183.

> **EXAMPLE**
>
> **Team 1:** What number comes after 12?
> **Team 2:** *Thirteen.*
> **Team 1:** What's the opposite of *tall?*
> **Team 2:** *Short.*

7 DIALOGUES

A. Listen to the dialogues. Write the word you hear in the blank.

1. **A:** Do you remember your _____ love?

   B: Oh, yes! His name was Rick Moore.

   A: Do you still _____ him?

   B: No, he moved away and we lost touch.*

2. **A:** Do you _____ your first teacher?

   B: Oh, yes. Mrs. Rinaldo. I'll _____ _____ her!

   A: You didn't like her?

   B: No! And she didn't like me!

3. **A:** Do you remember your first _____?

   B: I never had a car. I don't know how to drive.

4. **A:** Do you remember your first job?

   B: Of course. I still have it.

      I'm an _____ _____ .

B. Work with a partner. Check your answers. Then practice the dialogues in Part A.

---

* *lost touch*: don't know each other now

Work with a partner. Talk about some of your "firsts," such as your first teacher, job, love, car, friend, home. Use the dialogues in Exercise 7 for ideas. Write the information below.

Partner's Name

My partner's first

ON YOUR OWN

🎧 **First listen to:**

- the words in Exercises 1, 2, and 3.
- the sentences in Exercise 5.

📼 **Now record them.**

Self-Study: See page 152.

PART

2

CONSONANTS

INTRODUCTION

Consonant sounds are made by moving parts of the mouth close together.

1. Label the parts of the mouth. Use the words in the box.

| nose | lips | teeth | vocal cords | tongue |

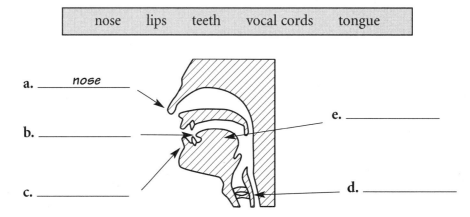

a. _____nose_____

b. _____

c. _____

d. _____

e. _____

2. Label the parts of the tongue. Use the words in the box.

| tip | middle | back |

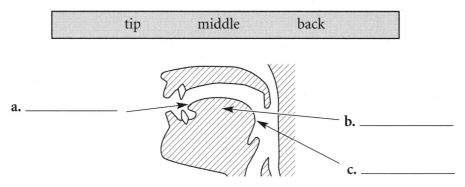

a. _____

b. _____

c. _____

FOCUSED PRACTICE

I CONSONANTS YOU CAN SEE

A. Look at the pictures on the next page. They show you how to use your mouth to say these six consonant sounds.

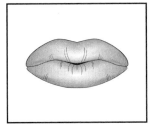
[p, b, m]

[f, v]

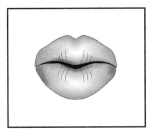
[w]

 B. Listen to these words and repeat them.

1. pie
2. bike
3. money

4. fish
5. fire
6. vest

7. west
8. water
9. window

C. Work with a partner. Take turns reading the words from Part B. Does your mouth look like the pictures in Part A?

2 CONSONANTS WITH A PUFF OF AIR

A. When [p], [t], or [k] begins a word, say the sound with a strong puff of air.

B. Listen to these words and repeat them. Say the first sound with a puff of air.

1. pay
2. park

3. time
4. tall

5. kiss
6. coat

3 VOICED AND VOICELESS CONSONANTS

A. [z] is a voiced sound. The vocal cords vibrate.

Say it: [zzzzzzzzzzzzzzzzzzzz]

B. [s] is a voiceless sound. The vocal cords do not vibrate.

Say it: [sssssssssssssssssssssss]

C. Put your fingers against your neck and make these sounds.

[zzzzzzz]   [sssssss]

Now put your fingers on your neck and feel the voicing go "on" and "off."

[zzzzzzz-sssssss-zzzzzzz-sssssss]

[vvvvvvvffffffffffvvvvvvvvffffffff]

4   FINAL CONSONANTS

A. Final consonant + vowel: a good answer

🎧 Listen to these words and repeat them. Join the final consonant to the next vowel.

1. Stop it!   3. Miss Adams   5. post office
2. Come on!   4. Ask a question. 6. a red apple

B. Final consonant + consonant (same consonants): five vans

🎧 Listen to these words and repeat them. Make one long consonant.

1. a big girl   3. I love Vicky!   5. call later
2. a black car   4. a red dress   6. a good dinner

C. Final consonant + consonant (different consonants): hot weather

🎧 Listen to these words and repeat them. Say the final consonant, but keep it short (" ' "). Then say the next consonant clearly.

1. a book' bag   3. Stop' singing!   5. white' pants
2. a big' dog   4. watch' TV   6. five' children

5   DIALOGUES

🎧 A. Listen to the recording and write phrases from Activity 4 in the blanks.

1. **Franz:** Is that your _____ _____ over there?
   Omar: No. I'm parked next to the _____ _____.

2. **Young:** I haven't had a _____ _____ for a long time.
   Jay: Me neither. I usually just open a bag of chips and _____ _____.

3. **Joyce:** Did anyone turn in a blue _____ _____?
   I lost mine today.
   Ms. Adams: Not yet. But _____ _____ and check again. The number is 845-6878.

B. Work with a partner. Practice reading the dialogues. Join the words in the blanks together.

UNIT 8 [θ] three and [ð] this

INTRODUCTION

Look at the picture. It shows you how to say the sounds of [θ] and [ð].

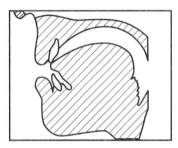

[θ] **three**   [ð] **this**

Put the tip of your tongue between your teeth to make the *th* sounds [θ] and [ð].

[θ] is voiceless.   [ð] is voiced.

Spelling for [θ] and [ð]: **three**, **this**, **mother**
Spelling, sound, and grammar

Nouns [θ]	Verbs [ð]
bath	to bathe
breath	to breathe

FOCUSED PRACTICE

▌ LISTEN AND PRACTICE: *Words with* [θ]

🎧 **A.** Listen to these words and repeat them. Put the tip of your tongue between your teeth.

1. think	5. thumb	9. mouth
2. Thursday	6. thousand	10. bath
3. throw	7. healthy	11. fifth
4. thin	8. something	12. teeth

B. Choose four words from Part A and write them on the lines.

Your words:

_____ _____ _____ _____

C. Work with a partner. Read your words to your partner. Your partner will write what you say. Then listen to your partner's words. Write them on the lines.

Partner's words:

_____ _____ _____ _____

2 LISTEN AND PRACTICE: *Words with* [ð]

A. Listen to these words and repeat them. Put the tip of your tongue between your teeth.

1. there	**5.** brother	**9.** clothing
2. that	**6.** feather	**10.** together
3. then	**7.** other	**11.** mother
4. those	**8.** father	**12.** breathe

B. Choose four words from Part A and write them on the lines.

Your words:

_____ _____ _____ _____

C. Work with a partner. Read your words to your partner. Your partner will write what you say. Then listen to your partner's words. Write them on the lines.

Partner's words:

_____ _____ _____ _____

3 GAME: [θ] *and* [ð]

Play this game in two teams—Team 1 and Team 2.

Team 1: Ask the questions on page 181 to the players on Team 2.

Team 2: Answer the questions with a word that has a th sound. Then ask Team 1 the questions on page 183.

4 HOLIDAYS: *Ordinal numbers*

A. Listen to the holiday names in column A and repeat them.

A	B
_d_ 1. Valentine's Day	**a.** a day for workers
___ 2. Christmas	**b.** the birthday of the United States
___ 3. Halloween	**c.** a day to wear costumes
___ 4. Memorial Day	**d.** a day to show your love
___ 5. Labor Day	**e.** a day of gift-giving and religious celebration
___ 6. New Year's Eve	**f.** the day to remember people who died in wars
___ 7. April Fool's Day	
___ 8. New Year's Day	**g.** the last night of the year
___ 9. Independence Day	**h.** the first day of the new year
___ 10. Thanksgiving Day	**i.** a day to give thanks
	j. a day for tricks and jokes

B. Work with a partner. Match the holidays in column A with the descriptions in column B. You can check your answers on page 180.

C. Work with a partner. Do you know the dates of the holidays in Part A? On the next page, write the holidays next to the dates. You can check your answers on page 180.

[θ] THREE AND [ð] THIS   39

1. December 25th _____ 7. February 14th _____

2. October 31st _____ 8. July 4th _____

3. December 31st _____ 9. the third Thursday of

4. April 1st _____   November _____

5. the last Monday of   10. the first Monday of

   May _____   September _____

6. January 1st _____

5 INTERVIEWS: *What's your favorite holiday?*

Work with a partner. Talk about your favorite holidays. Does your partner's country celebrate some of the holidays in Exercise 4?

EXAMPLE

What's your favorite holiday?

What do you do on _____ ?

Do you celebrate _____ in your country?

ON YOUR OWN

🎧 **First listen to:**

• the words in Exercises 1 and 2.

📼 **Now record them.**

Then record your answers to these questions using complete

sentences.

1. What's your favorite holiday?

2. When is it?

3. What do you do?

4. Why is it your favorite?

Self-Study: See page 153.

UNIT 9 [p] pen, [b] boy, [f] foot, [v] very, and [w] wet

INTRODUCTION

Look at the pictures. They show you how to say the sounds [p], [b], [f], [v], and [w].

pen [p]   **foot** [f]   **wet** [w]
boy [b]   **very** [v]
[p] is voiceless.   [f] is voiceless.
[b] is voiced.   [v] is voiced.

Spellings for [p]	Spellings for [b]	Spellings for [w]
people, put, keep	boy, baby	wet, west, well question, quiet
	Silent *b*  comb, bomb	Silent *w* write, wrong answer

Spellings for [f]	Spellings for [v]

Common
  fast, office, life
 	
Other
  phone, photo 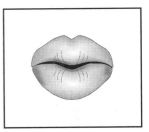
  laugh, cough
	very, love, never

Spelling, sound, and grammar	
Singular [f]	**Plural [v]**
a knife	knives
a leaf 	leaves

FOCUSED PRACTICE

1 LISTEN AND PRACTICE: *Words with* [p] *and* [b]

A. Listen to these words and repeat them.

	[p]				[b]		
1.	police	5.	happy	9.	box	13.	somebody
2.	paper	6.	open	10.	bank	14.	about
3.	picture	7.	stop	11.	book	15.	job
4.	play	8.	sleep	12.	blue	16.	robe

B. Choose four words from Part A and write them on the lines.

Your words:

_____ _____ _____ _____

C. Work with a partner. Read your words to your partner. Your partner will write what you say. Then listen to your partner's words. Write them on the lines.

Partner's words:

_____ _____ _____ _____

2 LISTEN AND PRACTICE: *Words with* [f] *and* [v]

A. Listen to these words and repeat them.

	[f]				[v]		
1.	five	5.	coffee	9.	van	13.	evening
2.	family	6.	elephant 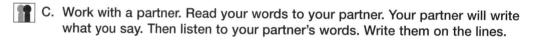	10.	visit	14.	seven
3.	foot	7.	knife	11.	vacation	15.	love
4.	phone	8.	laugh	12.	never	16.	arrive

B. Choose two [f] words and two [v] words from Part A and write them on the lines.

Your words:

_____   _____   _____   _____

C. Work with a partner. Read your words to your partner. Your partner will write what you say. Then listen to your partner's words. Write them on the lines.

Partner's words:

_____   _____   _____   _____

3 LISTEN AND PRACTICE: *Words with* [w]

A. Listen to these words and repeat them.

1. west	4. weather	7. quiet
2. water	5. away	8. language
3. winter	6. awake	9. question

B. Choose four words from Part A and write them on the lines.

Your words:

_____   _____   _____   _____

C. Work with a partner. Read your words to your partner. Your partner will write what you say. Then listen to your partner's words. Write them on the lines.

Partner's words:

_____   _____   _____   _____

A. Listen to these words and repeat them.

1. **a.** co<u>p</u>y

   b. <u>c</u>offee

2. **a.** <u>p</u>ear

   b. <u>f</u>air

3. **a.** <u>f</u>erret

   b. <u>p</u>arrot

4. **a.** <u>f</u>ox

   b. <u>b</u>ox

5. **a.** <u>v</u>ote

   b. <u>b</u>oat

6. **a.** <u>v</u>est

   b. <u>w</u>est

7. **a.** <u>v</u>ery

   b. <u>b</u>erry

8. **a.** <u>V</u>

   b. <u>w</u>e

B. Listen again. Which word from Part A do you hear? Circle *a* or *b*.

C. Look at the words in Part A. Write each word under the correct picture.

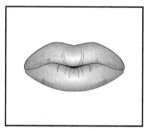 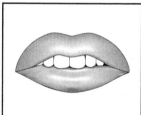 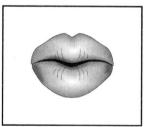

       copy

D. Work with a partner. Say the words under each picture in Part C. Does your mouth look like the picture?

🎧 **A. Listen to these sentences and repeat them.**

1. a. The fox is on the box.   **b.** The box is on the fox.

2. a. The ferret is in the cage.   **b.** The parrot is in the cage.

3. a. My money's in the west.   **b.** My money's in the vest.

4. a. The copy is under the coffee.   **b.** The coffee is under the copy.

🎧 **B. Listen again. Which sentence from Part A do you hear? Circle *a* or *b*.**

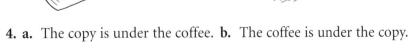

C. Work with a partner. Take turns reading a sentence from Part A. Your partner will point to the sentence you said.

6 GAME: [p], [b], [f], [v], *or* [w]

Play this game in two teams—Team 1 and Team 2.

Team 1: Ask the questions on page 181 to the players on Team 2.

Team 2: Answer the questions with a word that has [p], [b], [f], [v], or [w]. Then ask Team 1 the questions on page 183.

EXAMPLE

What animals fly?

Birds!

7 LISTENING: *Pets*

A. Listen to the words. Make sure you understand them.

popular pets	rabbits	pigs	snakes	bite
disease	responsibility	protect	bark	lonely

B. Read these questions.

1. What's the most popular pet in the United States?
2. What are some other common pets?
3. What are some unusual pets?
4. What are some problems with pets?
5. How can pets help us?

C. Listen to the recording. Then answer the questions in Part B.

8 INTERVIEWS: *Do you have a pet?*

Work in groups of three. Ask your group about their pets. Write answers in the chart.

	Name	Name	Name
Do you have a pet?			
Did you have a pet when you were a child?			
What kind of pet do/did you have?			
What kinds of pets are popular in your country?			
Do you like animals? Why or why not?			

ON YOUR OWN

🎧 **First listen to:**

• the words in Exercises 1, 2, and 3.

• the sentences in Exercise 5.

▣▣ **Now record them.**

Then make a one-minute recording about pets. You can talk about your own pet or pets in your country.

Self-Study: See page 154.

[s] s̲un, [z] z̲oo, [ʃ] s̲hoe, and [ʒ] televi̲sion

INTRODUCTION

Look at the pictures. They show you how to say the sounds [s], [z], [ʃ], and [ʒ].

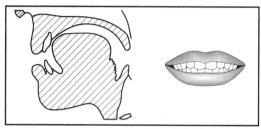

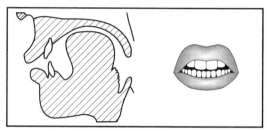

s̲un [s], **zero** [z]

Put the tip of your tongue high, behind your top teeth.

[s] is voiceless; [z] is voiced.

s̲hoe [ʃ], **televi̲sion** [ʒ]

Pull back your tongue. Round your lips a little.

[ʃ] is voiceless; [ʒ] is voiced.

Spellings for [s]	Spellings for [ʃ]
Common	Common
sun, sister, stop	shoe, wash, pushing
class, kiss, lesson	vacation, education
city, police, face	
Other	Other
house, horse	special, musician
scissors	sure, sugar
box, explain (x is [ks])	Chicago, machine
	ocean
Spellings for [z]	**Spellings for [ʒ]**
Common	Common
zoo, zero	television, decision, Asia
easy, visit, music	usually, unusual, pleasure
please, because	
Other	Other
scissors	garage

FOCUSED PRACTICE

1 LISTEN AND PRACTICE: *Words with* [s] *and* [z]

A. Listen to these words and repeat them.

[s]   [z]

1. sorry	5. bus	9. zoo	13. business
2. city	6. police	10. zebra	14. music
3. summer	7. answer	11. easy	15. please
4. face	8. listen	12. visit	16. rose

B. Choose four words from Part A and write them on the lines.

Your words:

_____ _____ _____ _____

C. Work with a partner. Read your words to your partner. Your partner will write what you say. Then listen to your partner's words. Write them on the lines.

Partner's words:

_____ _____ _____ _____

2 LISTEN AND PRACTICE: *Words with* [ʃ] *and* [ʒ]

A. Listen to these words and repeat them.

[ʃ]   [ʒ]

1. shoe	5. ocean	9. usually	13. treasure
2. shirt	6. vacation	10. pleasure	14. garage
3. wash	7. sugar	11. decision	15. television
4. machine	8. push	12. unusual	16. Asia

B. Choose two [ʃ] words and two [ʒ] words from Part A and write them on the lines.

Your words:

_____ _____ _____ _____

C. Work with a partner. Read your words to your partner. Your partner will write what you say. Then listen to your partner's words. Write them on the lines.

Partner's words:

_____   _____   _____   _____

3 LISTEN FOR DIFFERENCES: [s] vs. [z]

A. Listen to these words and repeat them.

1. **a.** a racer **b.** a razor

2. **a.** sea **b.** Z

3. **a.** Ross **b.** Roz

4. **a.** place **b.** plays

5. **a.** Sue **b.** zoo

6. **a.** price **b.** prize

7. **a.** lacy **b.** lazy

8. **a.** peace **b.** peas

B. Listen again. Which word from Part A do you hear? Circle *a* or *b*.

C. Work with a partner. Take turns reading a word from Part A. Your partner will point to the word you said.

A. Listen to these phrases and repeat them. Group the words together.

1. at the bus station
2. in a museum
3. an unusual show
4. a short vacation

5. in a garage
6. Ms. Oliver
7. on a cruise ship
8. at a zoo

9. in Asia
10. on television
11. at the seashore
12. December first

B. The underlined letters in Part A have [s], [z], [ʃ], and [ʒ] sounds. Write each word in the correct column. (Some words go in more than one column.)

[s]	[z]	[ʃ]	[ʒ]
bus			

C. Work with a partner. Compare your answers in Part B.

D. Write answers to these questions. Use phrases from Part A.

1. Where can you watch the news? *on television*
2. Where can you park a car? _____
3. Where is Thailand? _____
4. Where can you see famous art? _____
5. How can you get to Alaska? _____
6. Where can you see zebras? _____
7. What day follows November 30? _____
8. Where can you find seashells? _____
9. Where can you catch a bus? _____

E. Work in small groups. Take turns asking and answering the questions in Part D.

Different colors of roses have different meanings. When you send someone roses, you should be sure the color says what you want it to.

A. Listen to the words and repeat them. Make sure you know what the words mean.

1. roses
2. purity
3. bride
4. happiness

5. admiration
6. congratulations
7. unity

B. Look at the words with underlined letters. The underlined letters are pronounced [s], [z], or [ʃ]. Write the words on the lines below, matching the underlined letter with the pronunciation.

Pronunciation

[s] _____

[z] _____

[ʃ] _____

C. Listen to the recording. You will hear what different colors of roses mean. Write the meaning in the blank.

Color

Red roses _____

White roses _____

Yellow roses _____

Light pink roses _____

Dark pink roses _____

Orange roses _____

Red and yellow roses _____

Red and white roses _____

D. Choose a color. Tell the class what it means.

E. Work with a partner. Have you ever given roses to anyone? To whom? Did you send the right color?

ON YOUR OWN

🎧 **First listen to:**
- the words in Exercises 1 and 2.
- the phrases in Exercise 4.

📼 **Now record them.**

Self-Study: See pages 154–155.

UNIT 11 — [tʃ] chair and [dʒ] jet; [dʒ] jet and [y] yet

INTRODUCTION

Look at the pictures. They show you how to say the sounds [tʃ], [dʒ], and [y].

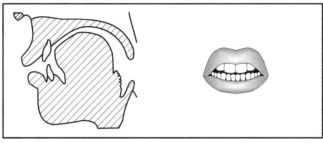

chair

[tʃ] starts as a *t* sound.
[tʃ] is voiceless.

jet

[dʒ] starts as a *d* sound.
[dʒ] is voiced.

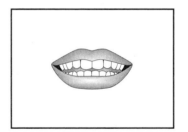

[y] **yet**

Spellings for [tʃ]	Spellings for [dʒ]	Spellings for [y]
Common	Common	Common
chair, chicken,	job, June, just	yes, young,
much	George, age	yellow
kitchen,	engine,	
watch,	imagination	
catch	bridge, judge	
Other	Other	Other
future	education,	university,
question	graduate	United States, U

FOCUSED PRACTICE

I **LISTEN AND PRACTICE:** *Words with* [tʃ] *and* [dʒ]

🎧 A. Listen to these words and repeat them.

	[tʃ]			[dʒ]
1. child	5. kitchen	9. jacket	13. education
2. church	6. question	10. job	14. engine
3. picture	7. catch	11. Jeep	15. college
4. chicken	8. lunch	12. January	16. bridge

B. Choose two [tʃ] words and two [dʒ] words from Part A. Write them on the lines.

Your words:

_____ _____ _____ _____

👥 C. Work with a partner. Read your words to your partner. Your partner will write what you say. Then listen to your partner's words. Write them on the lines.

Partner's words:

_____ _____ _____ _____

2 **LISTEN AND PRACTICE:** *Words with* [y] *and* [dʒ]

🎧 A. Listen to these words and repeat them.

	[y]			[dʒ]
1. yes	5. United States	9. jail	13. jaw
2. year	6. young	10. Jack	14. jet
3. yet	7. university	11. jar	15. jeans
4. yard	8. yellow	12. June	16. Jim

B. Choose two [y] words and two [dʒ] words from Part A. Write them on the lines.

Your words:

_____ _____ _____ _____

C. Work with a partner. Read your words to your partner. Your partner will write what you say. Then listen to your partner's words. Write them on the lines.

Partner's words:

_____ _____ _____ _____

3 LISTEN FOR DIFFERENCES: [y] *vs.* [dʒ], [ʃ] *vs.* [tʃ]

A. Listen to these words and repeat them.

1. a. Yale		**b.** jail	
2. a. wash		**b.** watch	
3. a. sheep		**b.** cheap	
4. a. potato ships		**b.** potato chips	
5. a. mush		**b.** much	
6. a. yes		**b.** Jess	
7. a. catch		**b.** cash	
8. a. share		**b.** chair	

B. Listen again. Which word from Part A do you hear? Circle *a* or *b*.

C. Work with a partner. Take turns reading a word from Part A. Your partner will point to the word you said.

4 DIALOGUES

A. Listen to these dialogues and repeat them.

1. **Mr. Jester:** George, did they fix my jet yet?
   George: Yes, Mr. Jester—yesterday.

2. **Alice:** Where did you go in July?
   Elena: You know—Juneau . . . Juneau, Alaska.

   Juneau

3. **Mom:** How much mush did the baby eat?
   Dad: Not much. Bring some cheese. She's a cheese lover.

4. **Marco:** On my way to the gym, someone was throwing cash out the window. I caught some.
   Eva: How much cash did you catch?

5. **Husband:** Why don't you wash the dishes and I'll watch TV?

    Wife: I have a much better idea. You wash and I'll watch.

6.   **Luis:** What does yellow Jell-O™ taste like?

    Anna: Lemon, I think. Red Jell-O tastes like cherries.

 B. Work with a partner. Practice the dialogues in Part A.

---

5   LISTENING

 A. Listen to these words and phrases and repeat them. Make sure you understand all the vocabulary.

1. college graduates   6. non-college graduates
2. higher pay   7. the Midwest
3. healthy (healthier)   8. list
4. citizen   9. reason
5. vote   10. my first chance

 B. Read this question. Then listen and answer the question.

What are some reasons a college education is important?

---

6   INTERVIEWS: *Is education important?*

Work in small groups. Discuss these questions.

Why is a good education important?
Do most people in your country go to college?
Is it hard to get into college in your country?
Is college expensive?

First listen to:

- the words in Exercises 1 and 2.
- the dialogues in Exercise 4.

Now record them.

Self-Study: See page 156.

UNIT 12 [r] road and [l] love

INTRODUCTION

Look at the pictures. They show you how to say the sounds [r] and [l].

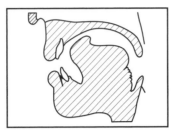

road [r]

Put the tip of your tongue up and back. Then move the tip of your tongue down. Don't touch the top of your mouth when the tongue moves down.

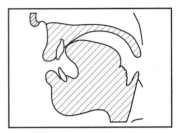

love [l]

Put the tip of your tongue behind the top teeth.

Spellings for [r]	Spellings for [l]

Common
   red, road
   arrive, sorry
Other (*w* is silent)
   write, wrong
	look, love, police
	hello, yellow

FOCUSED PRACTICE

I   LISTEN AND PRACTICE: *Words with* [r]

A. Listen to these words and repeat them.

1. right
2. rain
3. room
4. red
5. river
6. remember
7. sorry
8. arrive
9. parent
10. brown
11. drink
12. problem
13. street
14. green
15. tree
16. friend

B. Choose four words from Part A and write them on the lines.

Your words:

_____ _____ _____ _____

C. Work with a partner. Read your words to your partner. Your partner will write what you say. Then listen to your partner's words. Write them on the lines.

Partner's words:

_____ _____ _____ _____

2 LISTEN AND PRACTICE: *Words with* [l]

A. Listen to these words and repeat them.

1. light	**5.** late	**9.** color	**13.** slow
2. look	**6.** television	**10.** ceiling	**14.** blue
3. letter	**7.** family	**11.** clock	**15.** please
4. lemon	**8.** police	**12.** place	**16.** plate

B. Choose four words from Part A and write them on the lines.

Your words:

_____ _____ _____ _____

C. Work with a partner. Read your words to your partner. Your partner will write what you say. Then listen to your partner's words. Write them on the lines.

Partner's words:

_____ _____ _____ _____

3 LISTEN FOR DIFFERENCES: [r] *vs.* [l]

A. Listen to these words and repeat them.

1. **a.** road
   b. load

2. **a.** wrong
   b. long

3. **a.** fry
   b. fly

4. **a.** correct
   b. collect

5. **a.** arrive
   b. alive

6. **a.** pray
   b. play

7. **a.** pirate
   b. pilot

8. **a.** right
   b. light

B. Listen again. Which word from Part A do you hear? Circle *a* or *b.*

C. Work with a partner. Take turns reading a word from Part A. Your partner will point to the word you said.

4 LISTEN FOR DIFFERENCES: [r] *vs.* [l]

A. Listen to these sentences and repeat them.

1. **a.** Larry is collecting the papers. **b.** Larry is correcting the papers.

2. **a.** The children are praying. **b.** The children are playing.

3. a. Roland is a pirate.   **b.** Roland is a pilot.

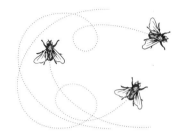

4. a. Those are fries.   **b.** Those are flies.

B. Listen again. Which sentence from Part A do you hear? Circle *a* or *b*.

C. Work with a partner. Take turns reading a sentence from Part A. Your partner will point to the sentence you said.

5 | DIALOGUE

A. Listen to the words and phrases. Make sure you understand all the vocabulary.

1. truthful

2. tell the truth

3. lie

4. article

5. haircut

6. awful

7. serious

8. hurt his feelings

B. Listen to this dialogue and repeat the lines. Group words together.

Ruth: Do you think you're a truthful person?

Leila: Of course! I always tell the truth! I don't lie.

Ruth: Well, last night I read an interesting article about lying.

Leila: What did the article say?

Ruth: It said most people tell about thirty lies a day.

Leila: Thirty? That's a lot. Well, I don't lie.

Ruth: Oh, really? Fifteen minutes ago, you told Tom you loved his new haircut. But when he left, you told me he looked awful.

Leila: Yes, but that's not a serious lie. That's a "white lie." I didn't want to hurt his feelings.

Ruth: But a white lie is still a lie. It's not the truth.

Leila: Maybe you're right. Today in class, I said I left my homework at home. But the truth is, I didn't do it.

C. Work with a partner. Practice the dialogue in Part B.

6 SITUATIONS: *Truth or lies?*

A. Make sure you understand these words and phrases.

a bright green tie	surprised	cheat

B. Now read these situations and dialogues.

In each dialogue, you can choose from three responses. One response is a lie (L). One response is the truth (T). One response is not a lie or the truth (N). Circle *L*, *T*, or *N* next to each response. Then choose the best response. Place a check (✓) after the response you would give.

1. **Situation:** Your friend is wearing a bright green tie. The tie looks awful.

   Friend: How does this tie look?

   You: (*L / T / N*) **a.** It's great! Really nice!

   (*L / T / N*) **b.** Awful! Your face looks green!

   (*L / T / N*) **c.** Is it new?

2. **Situation:** You're late for work because you didn't want to get out of bed.

   Boss: You're late. What happened?

   You: (*L / T / N*) **a.** Sorry. I didn't feel like getting up on time.

   (*L / T / N*) **b.** Sorry. I had a flat tire.

   (*L / T / N*) **c.** Sorry. Here's the report you wanted.

3. **Situation:** During a test, you cheated. You looked at a good student's answers and wrote them down. The next day, your teacher gives your test back.

   Teacher
   (surprised): You did very well on this test.

   You: (*L / T / N*) **a.** Oh, that's great!

   (*L / T / N*) **b.** I studied really hard for the test.

   (*L / T / N*) **c.** I cheated. I looked at my classmate's test.

 C. Work with a partner. Compare the letters you circled in Part B. Then practice the dialogues. Read each dialogue three times, each time with a different response.

ON YOUR OWN

🎧 **First listen to:**

• the words in Exercises 1 and 2.

📼 **Now record them.**

Then record a short story about a lie you told when you were a child.

Self-Study: See pages 156–157.

UNIT 13 [m] <u>m</u>outh, [n] <u>n</u>ose, and [ŋ] si<u>ng</u>

INTRODUCTION

Look at the pictures. They show you how to say the sounds [m], [n], and [ŋ].

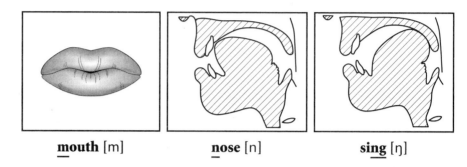

<u>m</u>outh [m]   <u>n</u>ose [n]   si<u>ng</u> [ŋ]

Spellings for [m]	Spellings for [n]	Spellings for [ŋ]
Common <u>m</u>ake, Ji<u>m</u> su<u>mm</u>er	Common <u>n</u>ow, ru<u>n</u> di<u>nn</u>er	Common bri<u>ng</u>, wro<u>ng</u>
Other co<u>mb</u>, bo<u>mb</u> (*b* is silent)	Other forei<u>gn</u>, si<u>gn</u> (*g* is silent) <u>kn</u>ow, <u>kn</u>ife (*k* is silent)	Other ba<u>n</u>k, thi<u>n</u>k

Spelling, sound, and grammar	
[ŋ] lo<u>ng</u> stro<u>ng</u> you<u>ng</u>	[ŋg] lo<u>ng</u>er stro<u>ng</u>er you<u>ng</u>er

FOCUSED PRACTICE

1 LISTEN AND PRACTICE: *Words with* [m] *and* [n]

A. Listen to these words and repeat them.

	[m]				[n]		
1.	meet	5.	Mom	9.	night	13.	nine
2.	movie	6.	remember	10.	knife	14.	run
3.	summer	7.	come	11.	dinner	15.	again
4.	family	8.	home	12.	tonight	16.	sun

B. Choose two [m] words and two [n] words from Part A and write them on the lines.

Your words:

_____   _____   _____   _____

C. Work with a partner. Read your words to your partner. Your partner will write what you say. Then listen to your partner's words. Write them on the lines.

Partner's words:

_____   _____   _____   _____

2 LISTEN AND PRACTICE: *Words with* [ŋ] *and* [ŋg]

A. Listen to these words and repeat them.

	[ŋ]				[ŋg]		
1.	sing	5.	wrong	9.	finger	13.	single
2.	singer	6.	bring	10.	longer	14.	younger
3.	song	7.	long	11.	stronger	15.	angry
4.	wing	8.	going	12.	English	16.	hungry

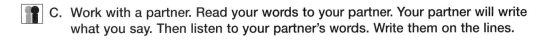

B. Choose two [ŋ] words and two [ŋg] words from Part A and write them on the lines.

Your words:

_____   _____   _____   _____

C. Work with a partner. Read your words to your partner. Your partner will write what you say. Then listen to your partner's words. Write them on the lines.

Partner's words:

_____ _____ _____ _____

3 JOIN WORDS TOGETHER: [m], [n], *and* [ŋ] + *vowel*

A. Listen to these sentences and repeat them. Join final [m], [n], and [ŋ] to the vowel that follows it.

1. What time is it?

2. His name is Mark.

3. Come in!

4. Bring it here.

5. Come back in a minute.

6. Call me in an hour. (*h* is silent)

7. Sing a song.

8. I'm going out.

9. Turn off the light.

10. She's watching a movie.

B. Choose three sentences from Part A and say them to the class.

4 DIALOGUE

A. Listen to these words and phrases. Make sure you understand all the vocabulary.

1. Congratulations!
2. promotion
3. Long Island
4. Sacramento

5. probably
6. India
7. New Delhi
8. reach someone by phone

B. It's 9:30 A.M. in New York City. At 9:00, Nancy's boss told her she got a promotion. John and Nancy are talking now.

Listen to the dialogue and repeat the lines. Group words together.

Congratulations.   Thank you.

John: Congratulations! I just heard about your promotion.

Nancy: Thanks. I'm really excited.

John: Have you told your family yet?

Nancy: Just my sister. She lives on Long Island. I called her a few minutes ago.

John: Your mom and dad are living in California, right?

Nancy: Yes, in Sacramento. But it's only 6:30 there. They're probably still sleeping. I'll call them later.

John: And your brother? He's working in India, isn't he?

Nancy: Yes. In New Delhi. It's hard to reach him by phone.

John: What time is it there?

Nancy: It's 7:30—at night. He's probably still working. He works long hours.

C. Work with a partner. Practice the dialogue in Part B.

---

5 **LISTENING:** *What time is it?*

A. Listen to these words and phrases, and repeat them. Make sure you understand all the vocabulary.

area	Pacific (Ocean)	Hawaii
Rocky Mountains	Midwest	Atlantic Ocean

B. Listen to the information. Then write the names of the time zones in the blanks at the top of the map. Write the times next to the cities.

_____ _____ _____ _____   _____

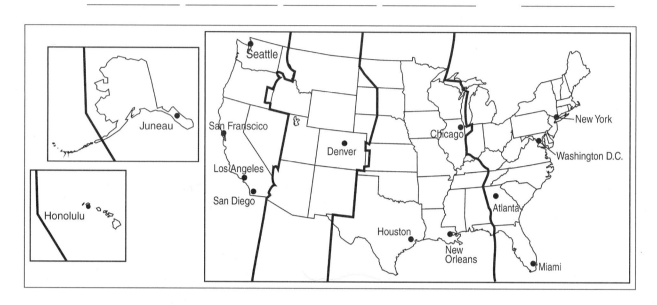

C. Look at the map. Choose a time and two places. Ask another student a question, using this model:

When it's _9 A.M._ in _Denver_, what time is it in _New York_?

6 WORLD TIMES

A. Look at the times for cities around the world.

4 A.M.	6 A.M.	7 A.M.	8 A.M.	12 noon	2 P.M.
• Los Angeles	• Chicago	• New York	• Sao Paulo, Brazil	• Madrid	• Istanbul, Turkey
• San Diego	• Mexico City			• London	

3 P.M.	5 P.M.		8 P.M.	9 P.M.	10 P.M.
• Cairo, Egypt	• New Delhi, India		• Beijing	• Tokyo	• Sydney, Australia
• Moscow				• Seoul	

B. Listen to these questions and repeat them. Join final consonants and beginning vowels.

1. When it's 5 P.M. in New Delhi, what time is it in Chicago?

2. When it's 7 A.M. in New York, what time is it in Sydney?

3. When it's 3 P.M. in Cairo, what time is it in Mexico City?

4. When it's 9 P.M. in Seoul, what time is it in San Diego?

C. Look again at Part A. Choose a time and two cities. Then work with a partner.

> When it's 9 P.M. in Tokyo, what time is it in Madrid?

> It's 12 noon.

D. Listen to these questions and repeat them.

1. When it's 5 P.M. in New Delhi, what are people in San Diego doing?
2. When it's 12 noon in London, what are people in New York doing?
3. When it's 10 P.M. in Sydney, what are people in Moscow doing?
4. When it's 2 P.M. in Istanbul, what are people in Madrid doing?

E. Listen to these *-ing* verbs and repeat them.

1. sleeping
2. having dinner
3. eating lunch
4. getting up
5. working
6. getting ready for work
7. going to work
8. watching TV

F. Work with a partner. Take turns asking and answering questions from Part D.

EXAMPLE

Student 1: When it's 5 P.M. in New Delhi, what are people in San Diego doing?

Student 2: They're probably *sleeping*.

ON YOUR OWN

🎧 **First listen to:**

- Exercises 1, 2, and 3.

▪️▪️ **Now record them.**

Self-Study: See pages 157–158.

Word endings: plurals and present tense

INTRODUCTION

- Use -s endings for . . .

Plural nouns	Present tense (third-person singular)
two boys, four books	She plays the piano.
Possessives	**Contractions of _is_ or _has_**
my mother's house	John's late.

- The -s endings have three pronunciations. The pronunciation depends on the last sound of the base word.

For words ending in . . .	pronounce the -s ending . . .	Examples
[s, z, ʃ, ʒ, tʃ, dʒ]	as a new syllable: [əz] or [ɪz]	roses He watches TV.
a voiceless sound: [p, t, k, θ, f]	as a final consonant: [s]	hearts Luke's here.
a vowel or a voiced consonant: [b, d, g, ð, v, m, n, ŋ, l, r]	as a final consonant: [z]	dogs Linda's house

FOCUSED PRACTICE

1 LISTEN AND PRACTICE: _Plurals pronounced_ [əz] / [ɪz]

🎧 A. Listen to these singular and plural words and repeat them.

	Singular	Plural		Singular	Plural
1.	bus	buses	**5.**	orange	oranges
2.	dress	dresses	**6.**	watch	watches
3.	prize	prizes	**7.**	box	boxes
4.	language	languages	**8.**	rose	roses

B. Listen again to the words in Part A. Tap the number of syllables with your finger when you repeat the words. Then underline the syllables.

EXAMPLE

bus   bus es

C. Choose three singular–plural pairs from Part A. Write them on the lines. Then work with a partner. Read your words to your partner. Your partner will write what you say.

Your words:

Singular	Plural
_____	_____
_____	_____
_____	_____

Partner's words:

Singular	Plural
_____	_____
_____	_____
_____	_____

2 LISTEN AND PRACTICE: *Plurals with* [s] *and* [z]

A. Listen to these singular and plural words, and repeat them.

Singular	[s] Plural	Singular	[z] Plural
1. cat	cats	5. dog	dogs
2. map	maps	6. boy	boys
3. student	students	7. pencil	pencils
4. bike	bikes	8. bed	beds

B. Listen again to the words in Part A. Tap the number of syllables with your finger when you repeat the words. Then underline the syllables.

EXAMPLE

cat   cats

C. Choose three singular–plural pairs from Part A. Write them on the lines. Then work with a partner. Read your words to your partner. Your partner will write what you say.

Your words:

Singular	Plural
_____	_____
_____	_____
_____	_____

Partner's words:

Singular	Plural
_____	_____
_____	_____
_____	_____

D. Apply the rule. How is the plural ending pronounced in these words? Write each plural noun in the correct column below.

1. nose
2. eye
3. night
4. horse

5. leg
6. book
7. office
8. town

9. peach
10. ship
11. week
12. job

[əz] / [ɪz]	[s]	[z]
_____	_____	_____
_____	_____	_____
_____	_____	_____
_____	_____	_____

A. Listen to the dialogue and repeat the lines. Group words together and speak smoothly.

Bill: I just met Anna Ross. She's great! What does she do?

Dragan: She works as a waitress during the day. At the Locust Tree.

Bill: Does she have a boyfriend?

Dragan: Why? Are you interested?

Bill: No, not really. Well, maybe a little.

Dragan: I don't think she goes out much. She's pretty busy. She has a night job too. She teaches dance at Steps Dance Studio.

Bill: Hmm. A dancer!

Dragan: Yeah. She wants to dance on stage someday.

Bill: What about weekends? Does she work then?

Dragan: I'm not sure. I think she gives private dance lessons on the weekend. She also practices new dances at Steps.

Bill: How does she get to Steps when she leaves the Locust Tree?

Dragan: She catches the bus in front of the restaurant. Why?

Bill: Maybe I'll give her a ride.

B. The underlined words in Part A have -s endings. How is the -s ending pronounced? Write each word in the correct column.

[əz] / [ɪz]	[s]	[z]
		she's

C. Work with a partner. Practice the dialogue in Part A.

4 JOBS AND ACTIVITIES

A. Listen to these verb phrases and repeat them. Make sure you understand all the vocabulary.

1. **Basketball**
   a. lift weights
   b. shoot baskets
   c. guard other players
   d. pass the ball

2. **Acting**
   a. memorize lines
   b. read scripts
   c. wear costumes
   d. work with a director

3. **President**
   a. give speeches
   b. live in the White House
   c. meet with other leaders
   d. travel to other countries

B. Write sentences under each picture to answer the question.

- Use the verb phrases from Part A.
- Use the present *-s* ending with the verbs. How is the *-s* ending pronounced?

1. What does a basketball player do?

He shoots baskets.

2. What does an actress do?

The king is here. The king is here.

3. What does the president do?

C. Work with a partner. Take turns asking and answering the questions in Part B.

🎧 **First listen to:**

- the words in Exercises 1 and 2.

▣▣ **Now record them.**

Then record some sentences about the leader of your country. Use present verb endings.

Self-Study: See page 159.

ON YOUR OWN

UNIT 15 Word endings: past tense

INTRODUCTION

The -ed ending has three pronunciations. The pronunciation depends on the last sound of the base verb.

For verbs ending in . . .	pronounce the -ed ending . . .	Examples
[t] or [d]	as a new syllable: [əd] or [ɪd]	paint—painted [t] [təd] land—landed [d] [dəd]
a voiceless sound: [p, k, θ, f, s, ʃ, tʃ]	as a final sound: [t]	wash—washed [ʃ] [ʃt] walk—walked [k] [kt]
a voiced sound: [b, g, ð, v, z, ʒ, dʒ, m, n, ŋ, r, l] or a vowel	as a final sound: [d]	listen—listened [n] [nd] try—tried [ay] [ayd]

FOCUSED PRACTICE

I **LISTEN AND PRACTICE:** *Past tense endings*

A. Listen to these present–past pairs and repeat them.

[əd] / [ɪd]	[t]	[d]
1. start—started	5. talk—talked	9. answer—answered
2. wait—waited	6. watch—watched	10. close—closed
3. need—needed	7. stop—stopped	11. enjoy—enjoyed
4. invite—invited	8. kiss—kissed	12. open—opened

B. Choose a pair from each column in Part A and write them on the lines.

Your words:

_____ _____ _____

C. Work with a partner. Read your pairs to your partner. Your partner will write what you say. Then listen to your partner's pairs. Write them on the lines.

Partner's words:

_____ _____ _____

D. Apply the rule. How is the past tense ending pronounced in these verbs? Write the past tense of each verb in the correct column below.

1. decide	4. work	7. push	10. rain
2. dance	5. stay	8. shout	11. paint
3. visit	6. laugh	9. happen	12. live

[əd] / [ɪd]	[t]	[d]
decided	_____	_____
_____	_____	_____
_____	_____	_____
_____	_____	_____

2 DIALOGUES

A. Listen to the dialogues and repeat the lines. Intonation is the music of your voice, the high and low notes. Follow the intonation lines. Join words together and speak smoothly.

1. **Rania:** You didn't finish your homework.

   Ming: Yes, I did. I finished it yesterday.

2. **Mike:** You didn't pay the phone bill.

   Sandra: Yes, I did. I paid it last week.

3. **Kumi:** You didn't like my party.

   May: Yes, I did. I liked it a lot.

B. Work with a partner. Practice the dialogues in Part A.

C. Work with a partner. Make up new dialogues, using these verbs and time words. Follow the example.

> **EXAMPLE**
>
> **Student 1:** You didn't *wash the car.*
> **Student 2:** Yes, I did. I *washed* it *this morning.*

1. **A:** answer my e-mail
   B: two hours ago

2. **A:** paint my mother's kitchen
   B: this morning

3. **A:** close your bank account
   B: yesterday

4. **A:** finish the book
   B: last night

3 | LISTENING

A. Listen to these words and phrases and repeat them. Make sure you understand all the vocabulary.

1. bus terminal
2. passenger
3. (to) head north
4. collect
5. charge someone money
6. fare
7. arrest

B. Listen to these past tense verbs and repeat them.

1. arrested	5. headed	8. repeated	11. stopped
2. charged	6. looked	9. returned	12. turned
3. collected	7. picked	10. started	13. walked
4. crossed			

C. How are the *-ed* endings in Part B pronounced? Write each verb in the correct column.

[əd] / [ɪd]	[t]	[d]
arrested		

D. Now listen to the "strange but true" story of a bus ride. Fill in the blanks with verbs from Part B.

A 20-year-old man _____walked_____ into the bus terminal in New York City. He got on a bus and sat down in the driver's seat. He _____ the bus and drove out of the terminal. He _____ north for the George Washington Bridge. On the way, he _____ at bus stops and _____ up passengers. He _____ them 50 cents for the ride. He _____ the bridge into New Jersey and _____ in Fort Lee. Then he _____ around and _____ to New York. He _____ his trip several times and _____ $88 in fares.

Finally, the police _____ him. They said he _____ just like a bus driver. His passengers said he was a good driver. They were surprised he wasn't a real bus driver.

E. Work with a partner. Tell the story of the bus driver. Make sentences with the past tense of these verbs. Take turns saying the sentences with your partner.

1. walk into the bus terminal
2. climb onto a bus, start the engine
3. head north for the George Washington Bridge
4. pick up passengers on the way
5. charge them 50 cents for the ride
6. cross the bridge into New Jersey
7. return to New York City
8. repeat the trip several times
9. collect $88 in fares
10. arrest the man

ON YOUR OWN

First listen to:
- the verbs in Exercise 1.
- the story in Exercise 3.

Now record them.

Then tell the story of the bus driver. Use the past tense of the verbs in Exercise 3E.

Self-Study: See pages 160–161.

INTRODUCTION

- Consonant groups with [r] and [l]

    Listen to the examples.

green	front	blue
drink	clock	play

- Consonant groups with [s]

    Listen to the examples.

ski	snow	stop
street	smoke	spring

- Consonant groups with [w]

    Listen to the examples.

question	quiet	swim
quickly	language	twelve

- Final consonant groups

    Listen to the examples.

dark	build	test
month	fix ([ks])	hand

- Grammatical endings can make new consonant groups.

    Listen to the examples.

stopped [pt]	skirts [rts]	listened [nd]
dogs [gz]	finished [ʃt]	fixed [kst]

- You can simplify the consonant groups in some words.

    Listen to the examples.

months (say "mənts")	clothes (say "(to) close")
fifths (say "fifs")	asked (say "ast"—make the s long)

FOCUSED PRACTICE

A. Listen to these words and repeat them.

1. brown	5. place	9. drive	13. clock
2. price	6. dress	10. three	14. cry
3. black	7. angry	11. great	15. floor
4. blue	8. climb	12. clothes	16. problem

B. Choose four words from Part A. Write them on the lines.

Your words:

_____ _____ _____ _____

C. Work with a partner. Read your words to your partner. Your partner will write what you say. Then listen to your partner's words. Write them on the lines.

Partner's words:

_____ _____ _____ _____

A. Listen to these words and repeat them.

1. school	7. street	13. snake
2. skate	8. speak	14. snow
3. stay	9. spring	15. slow
4. stop	10. small	16. swim
5. steam	11. smell	
6. strong	12. smile	

B. Choose four words from Part A and write them on the lines.

Your words:

_____ _____ _____ _____

C. Work with a partner. Read your words to your partner. Your partner will write what you say. Then listen to your partner's words. Write them on the lines.

Partner's words:

_____   _____   _____   _____

3 LISTEN AND PRACTICE: *Consonant groups with* [w]

A. Listen to these words and repeat them.

1. question
2. quickly
3. quarter
4. quietly
5. quick
6. Gwen
7. language
8. twins
9. between
10. twelve
11. swing
12. sweater

B. Choose four words from Part A and write them on the lines.

Your words:

_____   _____   _____   _____

C. Work with a partner. Read your words to your partner. Your partner will write what you say. Then listen to your partner's words. Write them on the lines.

Partner's words:

_____   _____   _____   _____

4 LISTEN FOR DIFFERENCES: *One consonant vs. consonant group*

A. Listen to these words and repeat them.

One Consonant	Consonant Group
1. a. sure	b. shirt
2. a. bell	b. belt
3. a. Stan	b. stand
4. a. wash	b. washed
5. a. sing	b. sink
6. a. bag	b. bags
7. a. like	b. liked

84   UNIT 16

8. **a.** watch   **b.** watched

9. **a.** star   **b.** start

10. **a.** walk ["*l*" is silent]   **b.** walked

B. Listen again. Which word from Part A do you hear? Circle *a* or *b*.

C. Work with a partner. Take turns reading a word from Part A and pointing to the word you hear.

5 DIALOGUES

A. Listen to the dialogues and repeat the lines. Pronounce all the consonants in the consonant groups. Group words together.

1. **Shirley:** Do you like my shirt?

   Max: Sure, Shirley. I love your shirt.

2. **Steve:** Stand up straight, Stan! You're slumping!

   Stan: I can't! I just walked twelve miles. I'm tired!

3. **Marsha:** Josh, I'm so sorry! I washed your watch in the wash.

   Josh: That's the third time this month!

4. **Clara:** Let's go climbing at Criker's Peak today.

   Clarence: No, today is too cloudy. And Criker's Peak is always crowded.

Criker's
Peak

B. Work with a partner. Practice the dialogues in Part A.

6 WORD GROUPS: *Joining words*

A. Review these rules.

- Final consonant + vowel: Join the words.

  read it

- Final consonant + same consonant: Make one long consonant.

  call Linda

- Final consonant + different consonant: Keep the final consonant short. Then say the next sound clearly.

  rose⁾garden

B. Listen to these phrases and repeat them.

1. look at art
2. watch a movie
3. send a package
4. answer it
5. wake up

6. eat tacos
7. walk quickly
8. give Valentines
9. take classes
10. watch races

11. close the door
12. wash clothes
13. drive slowly
14. shoot baskets
15. read books

C. Listen to these questions and repeat them.

1. What can you do at a racetrack?

_____

2. What can you do at a museum?

_____

3. What can you do at a theater?

_____

4. What can you do at the library?

_____

5. What can you do at the post office?

_____

6. What can you do at a taco restaurant?

_____

7. What should you do if you're late?

_____

8. What can you do on Valentine's Day?

_____

9. What can you do on a basketball court?

_____

10. What do you do when you come into your house?

_____

11. What do you do when the alarm clock rings?

_____

12. What can you do at a university?

_____

13. What do you do at a laundromat?

_____

14. What do you do when the phone rings?

_____

15. What do you have to do in a traffic jam?

_____

D. Answer the questions in Part C. Use the phrases from Part B.

 E. Work in small groups. Compare your answers to the questions in Part C. Then take turns asking and answering the questions.

🎧 **First listen to:**
- the words in Exercises 1, 2, and 3.
- the phrases in Exercise 6.

▱ **Now record them.**

Self-Study: See page 161.

STRESS, RHYTHM, AND INTONATION

17 Stress, rhythm, and intonation overview

INTRODUCTION

1 SYLLABLES

- A syllable is a small part of a word. You can tap the syllables of a word with your finger.

car   → 1 syllable

airport   → 2 syllables

apartment → 3 syllables

A. Listen to these words and repeat them. Tap the syllables on your fingers.

1. building	**5.** library	**9.** office building
2. city	**6.** parking lot	**10.** supermarket
3. country	**7.** hospital	**11.** basketball court
4. bus stop	**8.** swimming pool	**12.** subway station

B. Listen to these words and repeat them. How many syllables are there? Write the number of syllables.

1. post office ___

2. sidewalk ___

3. college ___

4. university ___

5. bus station ___

6. television ___

7. classroom ___

8. coffee shop ___

9. bridge ___

10. movie theater ___

2 STRESSED SYLLABLES

- Only one syllable in a word has strong stress.
- The vowel in a stressed syllable is long.
- The vowel in a stressed syllable is loud.

A. Listen to these words. Notice the stressed syllable in each word.

apártment office cóllege

B. Listen to these words and repeat them. Make the stressed syllable long and loud.

1. stúdent
2. ócean
3. búilding
4. péople

5. políce
6. arríve
7. todáy
8. toníght

9. tomórrow
10. Aláska
11. impórtant
12. compúter

3 UNSTRESSED SYLLABLES

- Most vowels in unstressed syllables are pronounced [ə] or [ɪ].
- Vowels in unstressed syllables are short.
- Vowels in unstressed syllables are not loud.

A. Listen to these place names and repeat them. Make the stressed vowel long. Pronounce unstressed vowels as [ə].

1. Bóston
2. Téxas
3. Dállas
4. Chína

5. Wiscónsin
6. Atlánta
7. Jamáica
8. Koréa

9. Flórida
10. Míchigan
11. Cánada
12. Pórtugal

B. Work with a partner. Look at the place names in Part A. Are they cities, states, or countries? Write each name in the correct column. You can check your answers on page 180.

Cities	States	Countries
Boston	_____	_____
_____	_____	_____
_____	_____	_____
_____	_____	_____
_____	_____	_____

C. Work with a new partner. Make short dialogues about the places in Part A. Do you know anything else about the places?

> **EXAMPLE**
>
> **Student A:** What's Boston?
>
> **Student B:** It's a city. I think it's in Massachusetts.

4 RHYTHM: *Word groups and joining*

- Pronounce words in a phrase together.
- Join final consonants to beginning vowels.

A. Listen to these sentences. Notice the word groups.

He lives in Alaska.

Read a book.

Do you like your apartment?

B. Listen to these word groups and repeat them.

1. watch a movie

2. in a minute

3. a good answer

4. She's an artist.

5. Los Angeles

6. My brother's at home.

7. Let's go to the beach.

8. Give it to Sam.

5 RHYTHM: *Weak words*

- Many grammar words are weak or unstressed.
- *And* is usually pronounced [ən].
- *Or* is usually pronounced [ər], like the *-er* ending in *teacher*.

A. Listen to these phrases. Notice the pronunciation of *and* and *or.*

bacon and eggs	coffee or tea
paper and pencil	large or small

B. Listen to these phrases and repeat them. Pronounce *and* as [ən] and *or* as [ər].

1. men and women
2. black and white
3. Mom and Dad
4. dinner and a movie
5. come or go
6. chicken or fish
7. good or bad
8. north or south

6 RHYTHM: *Important words*

- Make important words long and loud.
- Say important words on a high pitch (a high musical note).

A. Listen. Think about the important words in the sentences.

That book was great!   No, that book was awful!

B. Work with a partner. Use the ideas in the box to write dialogues. Follow the example and the dialogue in Part A.

book	restaurant	movie	cake
song	game	concert	TV show

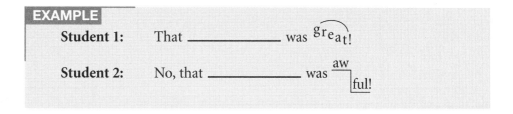

EXAMPLE

Student 1: That _____ was great!

Student 2: No, that _____ was awful!

7 INTONATION: *The music of your voice*

- English has higher high notes and lower low notes than some languages.
- Good intonation makes your meaning clearer.

A. Listen to these sentences and repeat them. Follow the lines when you say the sentences.

1. It's raining.

2. Good morning.

3. Thank you.

4. Is Lisa sick?

5. Where do you live?

6. Penguins can't fly!

7. Wait a minute.

8. Was the test easy?

B. Listen to these dialogues and repeat them. Notice how you can use your voice to give correct information.

1. **A:** Alaska's a city.

   B: No, it's a $^{s}ta_{t}e_{!}$

2. **A:** Boston's a state.

   B: No, it's a $^{ci}ty!$

3. **A:** Canada's a state.

   B: No, it's a $^{coun}try!$

4. **A:** California's a country.

   B: No, it's a $^{s}ta_{t}e_{!}$

C. Work with a partner. Practice the dialogues in Part B. Then write your own dialogues about places you know. Practice your dialogues.

UNIT 18 — Strong stress and secondary stress in words

INTRODUCTION

Strong Stress in Words

péople   tomórrow   Japán

- One syllable in each word has strong stress (′) .
- The vowel in a strong syllable is long.

Strong Stress in Two-Syllable Nouns

páper   péncil   stúdent

- Most two-syllable nouns have strong stress on the first syllable.

Strong Stress in Two-Syllable Verbs

vísit   ánswer   arríve   begín

- Some two-syllable verbs have strong stress on the first syllable.
- Some two-syllable verbs have strong stress on the second syllable.

Strong Stress (′) and Secondary Stress (`)

télevìsion   vàcátion   hómewòrk

- Some words have strong stress and secondary stress.
- Strong stress is the most important stress.
- Say syllables with strong stress on a high pitch: hómewòrk
- Say syllables with secondary stress on a lower pitch: hót dògs
- Syllables with secondary stress are longer than syllables with weak stress.
- Syllables with secondary stress are shorter than syllables with strong stress.

FOCUSED PRACTICE

LISTEN AND PRACTICE: *Strong syllables*

A. Listen to these words and repeat them. Make the strong syllables long.

1. dóctor
2. chíldren
3. ópen
4. próduct

5. todáy
6. políce
7. agáin
8. ánimal

9. Cánada
10. tomórrow
11. remémber
12. tomáto

B. Choose four words from Part A and write them on the lines.

Your words: _____   _____

_____   _____

C. Work with a partner. Read your words to your partner. Your partner will write what you say. Then listen to your partner's words. Write them on the lines.

Partner's words: _____   _____

_____   _____

2 **LISTEN AND PRACTICE:** *Hearing strong syllables*

A. Listen to these words and repeat them.

1. problem
2. tonight
3. address
4. banana
5. ocean

6. difficult
7. office
8. September
9. potato
10. Alaska

11. arrive
12. July
13. sister
14. o'clock
15. apartment

B. Listen to the words in Part A again. Which syllable has strong stress? Mark (" ′ ") over the stressed syllable.

EXAMPLE

próblem

C. Work with a partner. Compare your answers in Part B. Then write each word in the correct column.

Strong stress is on the . . .

first syllable	middle syllable	last syllable
problem		

D. Choose two words from each column in Part C. Write them on the lines. Then work in small groups. Take turns reading your words aloud. Make the strong syllable long.

first syllable	second syllable	last syllable

3 DIALOGUES

A. Do you know what these words mean?

delicious   fattening   greasy   popcorn   snack   sweet

B. Listen to these dialogues and repeat the lines.

1.   **Max:** Do you líke hámburgers?
     Sasha: Nó. They're too gréasy.

2.   **Alicia:** Whát do you líke for a snáck?
     Elena: I líke frúit. It's nót fáttening.

3.   **Zhang:** Do you líke pópcorn?
     Jin: Yés! It's delícious.

4.   **Lee:** Do you líke cándy bàrs?
     Tatsuya: Nó. They're too swéet.

C. Work with a partner. Practice the dialogues in Part B.

4 WORD GROUPS: *American snack foods*

A. Listen to these words and repeat them. Make syllables with strong stress (´) long. Say syllables with strong stress on a high pitch.

1. hámburgers	7. potáto chìps	13. ápples
2. hót dògs	8. tácos	14. pízza
3. sóda	9. cóokies	15. íce crèam
4. cándy bàrs	10. tortílla chìps	16. frénch frìes
5. prétzels	11. cárrots	17. banánas
6. pópcòrn	12. célery	18. yógurt

B. These words describe food. Listen to the words and repeat them. Do you know what the words mean?

1. greásy	5. héalthy	9. líght
2. sálty	6. unhéalthy	10. sóur
3. sweét	7. heávy	11. spícy
4. delícious	8. fáttening	12. áwful

C. Work with a partner. Look at each snack food in Part A. Is the food healthy, unhealthy, fattening, or light? Write the foods on the lines below. Do you agree about the foods you know?

> **EXAMPLE**
>
> **Student 1:** Are hamburgers healthy?
>
> **Student 2:** No, they're not. They're unhealthy and fattening.

Healthy _____

Unhealthy _____

Fattening _____

Light _____

D. What foods in Part A do you like? Write the snacks on one of the lines below. Then work in groups to compare opinions. Do you agree with other members in your group?

Delicious _____

OK _____

Awful _____

ON YOUR OWN

First listen to:
- the words in Exercises 1 and 4.

Now record them.

Then record a short description of your favorite snacks. Say why you like them. You can use words from Exercise 4.

Self-Study: See pages 162–163.

UNIT **19** Weak syllables in words

INTRODUCTION

Weak Syllables

ópen
[ə]

guitár
[ə]

Julý
[ə]

bácon
[ə]

- The underlined syllables in the words above are weak syllables. They are not stressed.
- Vowels in weak syllables are pronounced [ə] (or sometimes [ɪ]).
- Vowels in weak syllables are not long.
- Vowels in weak syllables are not clear.

Final Weak Syllables Ending in *ow, o, y, i*

yéllow
[ow]

potáto
[ow]

háppy
[iy]

táxi
[iy]

- The underlined syllables in the words above are weak syllables.
- Final weak syllables spelled *-ow/-o* are pronounced [ow].
- Final weak syllables spelled *-y/-i* are pronounced [iy].

FOCUSED PRACTICE

I LISTEN AND PRACTICE: [ə] *in weak syllables*

A. Listen to these words and repeat them. The spelling shows how the weak vowels are pronounced. Make the strong syllables long and clear.

1. əwáy

   awáy

2. tədáy

3. əgáin

4. pəlíce

5. dóctər

6. fáməs

7. Énglənd

8. próbləm

9. vísət

10. əpártmənt   12. ánəməl   14. əláskə

_____   _____   _____

11. təmórrow   13. bənánə   15. Áprəl

_____   _____   _____

 B. Work with a partner. Write the normal spelling of the words in Part A in the blanks. Then practice saying the words. Use [ə] for the weak vowels.

2 LISTEN AND PRACTICE: *Hearing stress patterns*

A. Listen to these words and repeat them. Pay attention to the stress patterns.

Stress pattern   **Example**

1. ′ ə   fá mous
                                 ə

2. ′ ə ə   él e phant
                               ə   ə

3. ə ′ ə   a párt ment
                            ə   ə

4. ə ′   ma chíne
                            ə

B. Listen to these words. Cross out the word with a different stress pattern.

Stress pattern   **Example**

1. ′ ə   famous, garden, to~~day~~, chicken

2. ′ ə   thousand, kitchen, horses, arrive

3. ′ ə ə   tomorrow, beautiful, difficult, visitors

4. ə ′ ə   Alaska, Canada, December, November

5. ə ′   o'clock, police, again, apple

3 WORD GROUPS: *Animals*

A. Listen to these words and repeat them.

1. elephants
2. giraffes
3. tigers
4. lions

5. zebras
6. buffalo
7. ostriches
8. pandas

9. leopards
10. camels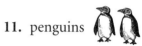
11. penguins
12. cobras

B. Listen to the words in Part A again. Mark the strong syllable (′). Write [ə] under the weak syllables.

EXAMPLE

élephants
[ə] [ə]

C. Work with a partner. Compare your answers in Part B. Then look at the animals again. In what parts of the world are these animals usually found? Write the animal names on the map.

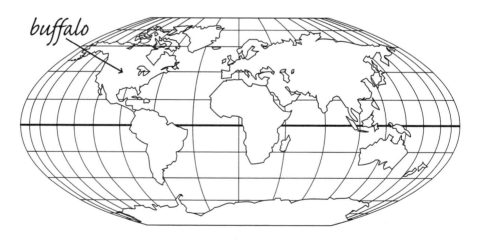

buffalo

D. Choose an animal from Part A. Tell the class where the animal is found.

> **EXAMPLE**
>
> Buffalo are found in North America.

4 DIALOGUES

A. These phrases describe animals. Listen to the phrases and repeat them, joining words together. Do you know what the words mean?

1. a wild animal
2. a domestic animal
3. a farm animal
4. a fierce animal
5. a gentle animal
6. a pet

B. Listen to these dialogues and repeat the lines. Join words together.

1. **Sam:** What's a hippopotamus?

   Jose: It's a wild animal.

   Sam: Where does it live?

   Jose: In Africa.

2. **Yuri:** What's an eagle?

   John: It's a very big bird. It's the national bird of the United States.

   Yuri: Where does it live?

   John: In mountains and forests.

3. **Rebecca:** What's a goat?

   Tony: It's a farm animal.

   Rebecca: Is it big?

   Tony: It's not too big. And it's not too small.

C. Work with a partner. Practice the dialogues in Part B.

5   GAME: *The Animal Name Game*

Play this game with the class.

Student 1:   Think of an animal.
Tell the class the first letter of the animal's name.

Class: Ask Student 1 questions about the animal.
Try to guess what the animal is.
You can use words and questions from Exercise 4.

> **EXAMPLE**
>
> **Student 1:**   This animal's name starts with c.
> **Student 2:**   Is it a wild animal?
> **Student 1:**   No.
> **Student 3:**   Is it a pet?
> **Student 1:**   Yes.
> **Student 3:**   Is it a cat?
> **Student 1:**   Yes!

ON YOUR OWN

🎧 **First listen to:**

- the words in Exercises 1 and 3.

📼 **Now record them.**

Then record descriptions of four animals. You can use ideas from Exercises 3 and 4.

Self-Study: See page 163.

UNIT 20 — Stress in compound nouns and numbers

INTRODUCTION

Compound Nouns (noun + noun)

drúgstòre   bús stòp   aírpòrt   boókstòre

- The first noun has strong stress and high pitch.
- The second noun has secondary stress and lower pitch.

Numbers

13 thirtéen   30 thírty   14 fourtéen   40 fórty   15 fiftéen   50 fífty

- *-teen* words: Use strong stress on the *-teen* syllable.
- You can stress the first syllable when the next word is stressed on the first syllable.
  1920 (níneteen twénty) $18 (eíghteen dóllars)
- *-ty* words: Use strong stress on the number syllable.

Numbers in Addresses

535 (five thirty-five) First Street

- Say the numbers in two groups.
- The last two numbers are in one group.
- Don't say *hundred*.

701 (seven oh one) Main Street

- When 0 comes before the last number, say *oh*.

5012 (fifty twelve) Morningside Drive

- Say four-digit address numbers in two groups.
- Don't say *thousand*.

100 (one hundred) Fifth Avenue
4000 (four thousand) Yakima Avenue

- When 0's follow the first number, say *hundred* or *thousand*.

continued

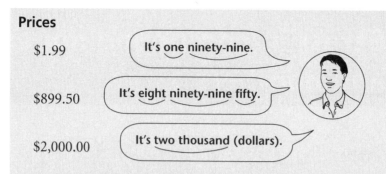

Prices

$1.99 — It's one ninety-nine.

$899.50 — It's eight ninety-nine fifty.

$2,000.00 — It's two thousand (dollars).

- We don't always say the words *dollars* or *cents*.
- Group the dollar words together.
- Group the cents words together.

FOCUSED PRACTICE

I. LISTEN AND PRACTICE: *Compound nouns*

A. Listen to these words and repeat them. Say the first word with strong stress and high pitch.

1. shoe store
2. post office
3. office building
4. bus stop
5. library book

6. grocery store
7. snowstorm
8. frying pan
9. bookstore
10. tennis courts

11. bedroom
12. backpack
13. desk lamp
14. park bench
15. dining room

B. Choose four compound nouns from Part A and write them on the lines.

Your words: _____ _____

_____ _____

C. Work with a partner. Read your words to your partner. Your partner will write what you say. Then listen to your partner's words. Write them on the lines.

Partner's words: _____ _____

_____ _____

1. a room for sleeping _____
2. a seat in a park _____
3. a place to play tennis _____
4. a place to buy stamps _____
5. a place to buy shoes _____
6. a storm with snow _____
7. a place to buy food _____
8. a book from the library _____
9. a room for eating _____
10. a pan for frying food _____
11. a place to catch a bus _____
12. a bag for carrying things _____
13. a lamp for a desk _____
14. a building with offices _____
15. a store for buying books _____

E. Look at the compound nouns in Part A. Write each compound noun next to the correct phrase in Part D.

F. Work with a partner.

Student 1: Ask a "what" question about a compound noun in Part A.
Student 2: Answer with a phrase from Part D. Use a complete sentence.
Then change roles.

> **EXAMPLE**
>
> Student 1: What's *a shoe store?*
> Student 2: It's *a place to buy shoes.*

A. Listen to these addresses in Pleasant Valley and repeat them.

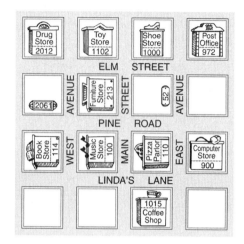

1. 2012 (twenty twelve) Elm Street
2. 1102 (eleven oh two) Elm Street
3. 1000 (one thousand) Elm Street
4. 972 (nine seventy-two) Elm Street
5. 2061 (twenty sixty-one) Pine Road
6. 1015 (ten fifteen) Linda's Lane

7. 900 (nine hundred) Linda's Lane
8. 114 (one fourteen) West Avenue
9. 100 (one hundred) Main Street
10. 213 (two thirteen) Main Street
11. 110 (one ten) East Avenue
12. 52 (fifty-two) East Avenue

B. Work in pairs. You both have maps of Pleasant Valley. Student 1 knows what stores are at some addresses. Student 2 knows what stores are at the other addresses. Ask each other questions until you both know what's at all the addresses.

Student 1: Look at your map on page 182. Ask your partner what's at the addresses with blanks. Write the answers in the blanks.

Student 2: Look at your map on page 184. Find the addresses Student 1 asks about. Tell Student 1 the answer. Then ask Student 1 questions about the blank addresses on your map.

EXAMPLE

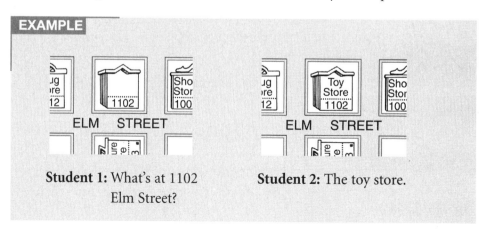

Student 1: What's at 1102 Elm Street?

Student 2: The toy store.

DIALOGUES

A. Listen to these dialogues and repeat the lines.

1. **Marta:** How much is a movie ticket?

   Clerk: $10 (ten dollars) for adults, $6.50 (six fifty) for children.

2. **Lee:** How much is a gallon of milk?

   Clerk: $3.09 (three oh nine).

3. **Felix:** How much is this sofa?

   Clerk: $999.99 (nine ninety-nine ninety-nine).

4. **Ana:** How much is this birthday card?

   Clerk: $2.95 (two ninety-five).

B. Work with a partner. Practice the dialogues in Part A.

ON YOUR OWN

First listen to:

- the compound nouns in Exercise 1.
- the addresses in Exercise 2.

Now record them.

Then record five addresses that you know. Use complete sentences.

EXAMPLE

My grandparents' address is 42 (forty-two) Calle San Isidro.

Self-Study: See page 164.

UNIT 21 — Strong words and weak words in sentences

INTRODUCTION

Strong Words in Sentences

> Men's Basketball — Feb. 8 — 8 P.M. School Gym

> There's a **MEN'S BAS**ketball **GAME** on **FEB**ruary **EIGHTH** at **EIGHT** P.M. in the **SCHOOL GYM.**

- Strong words in sentences have strong stress.
- Strong words have clear meanings.
- Strong words are easy to hear.
- Strong words are usually nouns, verbs, adjectives, and adverbs.

Weak Words in Sentences

> *Room for Rent*
> *Big, Good View, Quiet*

> I have a **ROOM** for **RENT**. It's **BIG**. It has a **GOOD VIEW**. It's **QUIET.**

- Weak words are often "grammar" words: *the, a, it, to, in.*
- Weak words are not stressed.
- Weak words are harder to hear.
- Signs and newspaper headlines often don't include weak words.

The Strongest Word

The room's for RENT. It's BIG. The rent's LOW.

- Usually one word in a sentence is strongest.
- The strongest word has the most important information.
- The strongest word is very easy to hear.
- The strongest word is often said on a high pitch.

FOCUSED PRACTICE

I LISTEN AND PRACTICE: *Strong and weak words*

A. Listen to these phrases and repeat them. Say the strong word clearly. Make the stressed syllable of the strong word long. Group words together.

1. in the SUMMER

   the BEACH

   to the BEACH

   GO to the BEACH

   She LIKES to GO to the BEACH.

   She LIKES to GO to the BEACH in the SUMMER.

2. the BUS

   on the BUS

   his WALLET

   He LOST his WALLET.

   He THINKS he LOST his WALLET.

   He THINKS he LOST his WALLET on the BUS.

B. Choose three phrases from Part A and write them on the lines.

Your phrases:

_____   _____   _____

C. Work with a partner. Read your phrases to your partner. Your partner will write what you say. Then listen to your partner's phrases. Write them on the lines.

Partner's phrases:

_____   _____   _____

2 LISTEN FOR DIFFERENCES: *Strong words vs. weak words*

Bulletin boards are places to put information. Other people can read your information on the bulletin board. José, Akiko, and Lenka want to put notices (signs) on the school bulletin board.

A. Listen to each person's information and repeat the sentences.

1. José's information
   a. I'm MOVING.
   b. I'm SELLING some FURNITURE.
   c. I'm SELLING a COUCH for $200.
   d. I'm SELLING a TABLE for $50.
   e. I'm SELLING FOUR CHAIRS.
   f. They're $20 EACH.
   g. Everything's in GOOD CONDITION.
   h. You can CALL me at 662-9045.

2. Akiko's information
   a. I WANT a BABYSITTING JOB.
   b. I'm a STUDENT at the COLLEGE.
   c. I LOVE CHILDREN.
   d. I'm AVAILABLE at NIGHT.
   e. You can CALL me at 710-1041.

3. Lenka's information
   a. I NEED a RIDE to CHICAGO.
   b. I WANT to GO in MID-DECEMBER.
   c. I'll SHARE the DRIVING.
   d. I'll SHARE the COST of GAS.
   e. You can CALL me at 687-7832.

B. Work with a partner. Complete the bulletin board announcements for José, Akiko, and Lenka. Use the information from Part A.

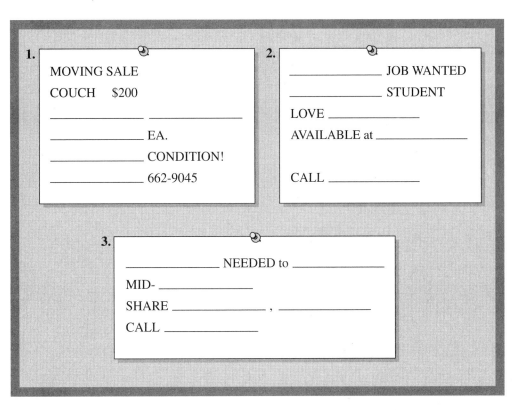

1.

MOVING SALE

COUCH $200

_____ _____

_____ EA.

_____ CONDITION!

_____ 662-9045

2.

_____ JOB WANTED

_____ STUDENT

LOVE _____

AVAILABLE at _____

CALL _____

3.

_____ NEEDED to _____

MID- _____

SHARE _____ , _____

CALL _____

C. Look at these bulletin board ads. Fill in the blanks below each ad to make complete sentences.

1.

CLASS PARTY

TONIGHT, 9 P.M.

MARY'S APT.

42 FIRST ST.

There will be a _____ _____ tonight at _____
P.M. The party's at _____ _____ . Her
address_____ 42 _____ _____ .

2.

ROOM for RENT
SMALL, SUNNY
CLOSE to BUS, $400/MO.
NON-SMOKER ONLY
CALL FRANCO 857-6765

I _____ _____ room for _____ . It's

_____ , _____ , and _____ to

_____ bus. The _____ is $400 a month. I only want

_____ _____-smoker. _____ Franco

_____ 857-6765.

3.

ENGLISH 1101
FINAL EXAM
DEC. 13, 9–11 A.M.
RM 202

The_____ _____ for English 1101 will

be_____ 13th, from _____ A.M. to _____ A.M.

The exam _____ be _____ Room _____.

4.

SOCCER TEAM PRACTICE
TODAY 4:30
WRIGHT'S FIELD

The _____ _____ will practice _____ at

_____ . Practice will be at _____ Field.

D. Work with a partner. Choose two announcements from Part C. Tell your partner what they say. Use complete sentences. Remember to give strong stress to important words.

A. Listen to the words and phrases in the box and repeat them. Make sure you understand all the vocabulary.

residence halls	lively	communities
develop interests	extracurricular activities	staff
academic achievement		Internet hookups
cable TV	lounges	

B. Listen to the information about residence halls at an American university. Fill in the blanks with the words you hear. Listen carefully. The missing words are weak words like prepositions (*in, of,* etc.) and articles (*a, an, the*).

More than 5,000 _____ our students call our residence halls home. _____ home _____ _____ lot more than _____ room _____ _____ bed. Our residence halls _____ lively communities. You'll make friends _____ have many opportunities _____ develop interests _____ all kinds _____ extracurricular activities. _____ staff _____ _____ residence halls cares _____ your academic achievement _____ _____ personal development.

There _____ cable TV _____ Internet hookups _____ every room. _____ every residence hall, there are lounges _____ exercise areas. Our residence halls _____ planned _____ help _____ study, relax, play, and feel _____ home.

C. Work with a partner. Compare answers in Part B. Then practice reading the paragraphs. Group words together. Say the weak words, but don't stress them.

First listen to:
- the phrases in Exercise 1.
- the sentences in Exercise 2.

Now record them.

Self-Study: See pages 165–166.

INTRODUCTION

The Most Important Word in a Sentence

I saw a **GREAT** movie   **GREAT**? It was **AWFUL!**

- In a sentence, one word is usually the most important.
- We "highlight" this word with very strong stress.
- We also highlight this word with high pitch (a high note).

Giving New Information in a Sentence

What's your name?   My name is **CHANG**.

- We highlight new information in a sentence.

Correcting and Contrasting Information

My flight doesn't leave at eleven. It leaves at **TEN**.

YOUR flight leaves at **ELEVEN**. **MINE** leaves at **TEN**.

- We highlight when we correct information.
- When we correct or contrast words, the correct information is the most important in the sentence.
- We highlight corrections and contrasting words.

FOCUSED PRACTICE

<table>
<tr><td>**1**</td><td>**LISTEN AND PRACTICE:** *Hearing the most important word*</td></tr>
</table>

A. Listen to these sentences and repeat them. You will hear each sentence three times. The speaker will highlight a different word each time.

1. I watched a French movie on TV last night.

   a. _____

   b. _____

   c. _____

2. My new computer isn't very fast.

   a. _____

   b. _____

   c. _____

3. I tried to call you at home this morning.

   a. _____

   b. _____

   c. _____

B. Listen again to the sentences in Part A. Which word does the speaker highlight? Write the highlighted words in the blanks.

<table>
<tr><td>**2**</td><td>**DIALOGUE**</td></tr>
</table>

Listen to the dialogue and repeat the lines. Circle the words that are highlighted.

Stella: I made a dentist appointment for you on Thursday.

Stanley: I don't need to see the doctor.

Stella: A dentist appointment, Stanley. The dentist.

Stanley: I can't go on Friday. I'm working.

Stella: I said Thursday. The appointment's for Thursday.

Stanley: I don't like Dr. Corkrum.

Stella: We haven't seen Dr. Corkrum for years! He's retired.

Stanley: Good. Because I never liked him.

Student 1: Read a numbered sentence to your partner.

Student 2: Ask the questions under Student 1's sentence.

Student 1: Answer the questions. Use your voice to highlight the correct information.

EXAMPLE

> **Student 1:** I went to a beach party with my roommate last weekend.
>
> **Student 2:** What kind of party did you go to?
>
> **Student 1:** A BEACH party.

1. I went to a beach party with my roommate last weekend.

   a. What kind of party did you go to?

   b. Did you go yesterday?

   c. Who did you go with?

   d. Did you say a beach concert?

2. My brother is a reporter for a newspaper in Seattle.

   a. Did you say your father is a reporter?

   b. He works in Boston?

   c. Did you say your brother's a photographer?

   d. Is he a reporter for a TV news program?

4 **LISTEN AND PRACTICE:** *Correcting information*

A. Listen to these sentences and repeat them. Each sentence has incorrect information.

   1. There are 58 minutes in an hour.
   2. There are 31 days in September.
   3. Miami is in Texas.
   4. The president of the United States lives in the Pink House.
   5. Water freezes at 10° (ten degrees) Centigrade.
   6. Chicago is a small city.
   7. Mexico is north of the United States.
   8. April is the third month of the year.
   9. A square has five corners.

10. A red traffic light means "Go."
11. Boston is a city in Canada.
12. There are 22 hours in a day.
13. The *Titanic* was a large bus.
14. Shakespeare was a famous Japanese writer.

 B. Work with a partner. Take turns reading a sentence from Part A and correcting the information. Remember to use your voice to highlight the correct information. (You can check your answers on page 180.)

> **EXAMPLE**
>
> **Student 1:** Paris is in ENGLAND.
> **Student 2:** Excuse me, but Paris is in FRANCE.
> **Student 1:** The weather's COLD at the equator.
> **Student 2:** That's WRONG. The weather's HOT at the equator.

C. Write three sentences that have incorrect information. Your sentences can be about people or places. Write incorrect information that your classmates will know is wrong.

1. _____

2. _____

3. _____

 D. Work with a partner. Take turns reading and correcting your sentences from Part C. Be sure to highlight the correct information.

🎧 **First listen to:**
- the sentences in Exercise 1.

▣▣ **Now record them.**

Then record the sentences in Exercise 4. Correct the information that is wrong, using your voice to highlight the correct words.

Self-Study: See pages 166–167.

UNIT 23 Common weak words

INTRODUCTION

And

- In speaking, *and* is a weak word.
- In speaking, *and* sounds like [ən].
- Join *and* to the word before it.
- We sometimes write *and* as *'n'* in signs.

Or

- In speaking, *or* is a weak word.
- In speaking, *or* sounds like the *-er* ending in *bigger*: [ər].
- Join *or* to the word before it.

Can

- *Can* is a weak word when a verb follows it.
- Pronounce *can* as [kən] when a verb follows it.
- Join *can* to the words around it.
- *Can* is a strong word in short answers: [kǽn].
  Yes, I cán.   Yes, he cán.

Can't

- *Can't* is always a strong word: [kǽnt].
  I cán't come.   We cán't do it.

FOCUSED PRACTICE

	LISTEN AND PRACTICE: *Phrases with* and

A. Listen to these words for some foods that often go together. Repeat the phrases. Pronounce *and* as [ən]. Join it to the first word.

1. surf and turf
2. turkey and stuffing
3. cookies and milk
4. bacon and eggs
5. bread and water

6. salt and pepper
7. cake and ice cream
8. chips and dip
9. fish and chips
10. rice and beans

B. Choose three phrases from Part A and write them on the lines.

Your phrases:

_____   _____   _____

C. Work with a partner. Read your phrases to your partner. Your partner will write what you say. Then listen to your partner's phrases. Write them on the lines.

Partner's phrases:

_____   _____   _____

D. Work in small groups. The foods in Part A are eaten by different groups of people or in different situations. Complete the sentences with the foods in Part A. (You can check your answers on page 180.)

1. In the Caribbean, it's ___*rice and beans*___ .
2. For breakfast, it's _____.
3. In prison in the old days, it was _____.
4. At beach restaurants, it's _____.
5. For a children's snack, it's _____.
6. For dessert, it's _____.
7. At a party, it's _____.
8. For Thanksgiving, it's _____.
9. These spices make food taste better: _____.
10. In England, it's _____.

E. Write down other foods that go together. Then tell your group about foods that often go together in your country.

> **EXAMPLE**
>
> We eat a lot of shrimp and vegetables.

2 LISTEN AND PRACTICE: *Phrases with* or

A. Listen to these phrases and repeat them. Pronounce *or* as [ər]. Join it to the first word.

1. married or single
2. one or two
3. right or wrong
4. chicken or steak
5. Saturday or Sunday
6. off or on
7. north or south
8. coffee or tea
9. cash or a check
10. chocolate or vanilla
11. hot or cold
12. left or right
13. in or out
14. March or April
15. cook or clean up

B. Choose four phrases from Part A and write them on the lines.

Your phrases: _____ _____

_____ _____

C. Work with a partner. Read your phrases to your partner. Your partner will write what you say. Then listen to your partner's phrases. Write them on the lines.

Partner's phrases: _____ _____

_____ _____

3 LISTEN FOR INTONATION: *Choices with* or

A. Listen to these questions and repeat them. Notice that when there are two choices, you say the first choice with rising intonation. You say the second choice with falling intonation.

1. Is it right or wrong?
2. Do I turn right or left?
3. Do I go north or south?

4. Do you want coffee or tea?

5. Are you married or single?

6. Do you want chicken or steak?

7. Do you want to stay in or go out?

8. Is it on Saturday or Sunday?

9. Do you want cash or a check?

10. Do you want chocolate or vanilla?

11. Is it in March or April?

12. Do you want to cook or clean up?

B. Listen again to the questions in Part A. Draw intonation lines (⌣ or ⌢) over the words joined by *or*.

4 LISTEN AND PRACTICE: can

A. Listen to the first part of these sentences and repeat them. Make *can* a weak word and join it to the pronoun before it.

1. I can _____.

2. You can _____.

3. He can _____.

4. She can _____.

5. We can _____.

6. They can _____.

B. Add verbs in Part A to make sentences. Then work with a partner. Compare your sentences. Practice reading your sentences. Make *can* a weak word.

5 LISTEN AND PRACTICE: can *and* can't

A. Listen to these sentences. Complete them with the words you hear: *can* or *can't*.

1. I _____ swim.

2. You _____ drive.

3. He _____ play the piano.

4. She _____ play soccer.

5. We _____ bring cake to the party.

6. They _____ play the drums.

7. I _____ dance, but I _____ swim.

8. I _____ speak Chinese, but I _____ speak German.

9. I _____ come on Saturday, but I _____ come on Sunday.

10. They _____ come early, but they _____ stay late.

🎧 **B.** Listen again to the sentences in Part A and repeat them.

 C. Write five sentences about things you can and can't do. Use the ideas in the box or your own ideas. Then work with a partner. Take turns saying your sentences.

Music:	play the piano, play the guitar, play the violin, sing
Sports:	swim, ski, golf, play basketball, play soccer, play tennis
Other:	drive, type, program a computer, cook, speak (language), dance

1. _____

2. _____

3. _____

4. _____

5. _____

ON YOUR OWN

🎧 **First listen to:**

- the phrases in Exercises 1 and 2.

- the questions in Exercise 3.

▪️ **Now record them.**

Then record your sentences from Exercise 5C.

Self-Study: See pages 167–168.

UNIT 24 | Contractions

INTRODUCTION

We usually use contractions—short forms of words—when we speak.

Contractions of *am, is, are*

I'm (= I am) 25.   She's (= She is) tired.

It's (= It is) raining.   You're (= You are) late.

We're (= We are) early.   He's (= He is) a doctor.

Contractions of *not*

I don't (= do not) like scary movies.

He isn't (= is not) here.

I can't (= cannot) come today.

They aren't (= are not) coming.

There is no contraction of *am not*.

Other Contractions

I'll (= I will) bring your book tomorrow.

I've (= I have) seen that movie.

He's (= He has) been sick for two days.

I'd (= I would) like a hamburger.

FOCUSED PRACTICE

1 | LISTEN AND PRACTICE: *Contractions*

A. Listen to these conversations and repeat the lines.

1. **A:** Let's hurry. We'll be late.
   B: Don't worry. We've got time.

2. **A:** They aren't home yet.
   B: They're probably stuck in traffic.

3. **A:** I've heard she's a professional skater.
   B: Really? I didn't know that.

4. **A:** I think you'll like this restaurant.
   B: I'm sure you're right.

5. **A:** We're leaving at 8:30.
   B: Don't worry. I won't forget.

6. **A:** She doesn't work here anymore.
   B: Do you have her phone number? I'd like to call her.

B. Work with a partner. Practice the conversations in Part A.

---

2 **LISTEN AND PRACTICE:** *Words that sound alike*

Listen to these sentences and repeat them. The underlined words are pronounced the same or almost the same.

1. Nick'll give a nickel.

2. I'll bring them all.

3. He'll climb the hill.

4. Mr. Peep'll meet people.

5. Rose's near the roses.

6. Mr. Loak'll take the local train.

7. Some are coming this summer.

8. Your price's higher than their prices.

---

3 **DIALOGUE**

A. Listen to this dialogue. Complete it with the contractions you hear.

Sam: Hello?

Lucy: Sam? It'____ me.

Sam: Where have you been? You'____ two hours late.

Lucy: It'____ a long story, Sam. I'____ tell you later. But now I'____ lost.
   And I'____ almost out of gas.

Sam: Where are you?

Lucy: I ____ know. I'____ at a gas station. I stopped to get gas, but it'____ closed.

Sam: What road are you on?

Lucy: Claremont, I think, but there'____ no sign.

Sam: What'____ across from the gas station?

Lucy: There'____ an old store—but I think it'____ closed. I ____ read the sign.

Sam: I think I know where you are. Did you pass a school a few miles back?

Lucy: Maybe. I ____ know. I ____ notice.

Sam: It'____ OK. I'____ pretty sure I know where you are. How much gas do you have?

Lucy: I'____ almost on empty.

Sam: OK. Stay there. You'____ too far away to drive. I'____ coming to get you.

Lucy: Please hurry. It'____ getting dark, and I'____ getting scared.

B. Work with a partner. Compare your answers in Part A. Then practice the dialogue.

4 TOP TEN: *Lost and found*

Every year billions of people ride the subways and buses in New York City. And every year, those people lose their property.

A. The items below are lost on the subways and buses more often than any others. Read the list.

1. backpacks
2. walkmen, discmen, radios
3. (eye)glasses
4. wallets and purses
5. cameras
6. keys
7. cell phones
8. watches
9. in-line skates
10. jewelry

B. Make sure you understand the words in the box.

(watch) band	wrist	notice	leather	cash
pocket	nylon	brand	wheels	

C. Listen to the recording. You will hear five people describe something they lost on the subway. The items are from the list in Part A. As you listen, write the name of the item on the blank and words to describe it in the boxes below.

1. _____

2. _____

3. _____

4. _____

5. _____

D. Work with a partner. Use your notes in the boxes to describe an item. Use contractions when you can.

ON YOUR OWN

🎧 **First listen to:**

- the conversations in Exercise 1.
- the sentences in Exercise 2.

▶️ **Now record them.**

Then record a description of something you've lost. Use contractions.

Self-Study: See pages 168–169.

UNIT 25 Word groups

INTRODUCTION

Group certain words together when you speak.

- A word group has a word with strong stress.
- A word group usually has words with weak stress.
- Say the words in a group together.

Some Common Word Groups

Article + Noun	Verb + Pronoun/Noun	Preposition + Noun
the book	call me	at night
a computer	read the book	on the table

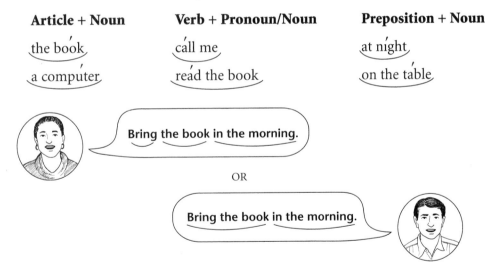

OR

- You can make groups in different ways.
- Don't put too many words in one group.
- Join the groups together this way: Hold the end of one group. Then start the next group.

FOCUSED PRACTICE

1 LISTEN AND PRACTICE: *Word groups with articles and prepositions*

A. Listen to these phrases and repeat them. Remember: Articles and prepositions have weak stress. Nouns have strong stress.

1. on the floor
2. in the car
3. at noon
4. on Sunday
5. before 6:00

6. to school
7. at home
8. to work
9. at 10:30
10. in a minute

11. for lunch
12. for my birthday
13. in summer
14. with a friend
15. in two thousand

B. Choose four phrases from Part A and write them on the lines.

Your phrases: _____   _____

_____   _____

C. Work with a partner. Read your sentences to your partner. Your partner will write what you say. Then listen to your partner's phrases. Write them on the lines.

Partner's phrases: _____   _____

_____   _____

2 LISTEN AND PRACTICE: *Word groups with verb + pronoun*

A. Listen to these sentences and repeat them. Remember: Verbs have strong stress. Pronouns have weak stress.

1. Visit me.
2. Ask her.
3. Buy it.
4. Throw it.
5. Stop it.

6. Call us.
7. Tell me.
8. Find it.
9. Watch it.
10. Open it.

11. Finish it.
12. Carry it.
13. Love me.
14. Take them.
15. Learn it.

B. Choose four sentences from Part A and write them on the lines.

Your sentences: _____   _____

_____   _____

C. Work with a partner. Read your sentences to your partner. Your partner will write what you say. Then listen to your partner's sentences. Write them on the lines.

Partner's sentences: _____ _____

_____ _____

3 LISTEN AND PRACTICE: *Hearing word groups*

A. Listen to these sentences. Underline the word groups.

1. Put it on the floor.
2. Bring them to work.
3. Meet me at the gym.
4. Throw it to Tom.
5. He called in the morning.

6. Come at 9:00 at night.
7. I heard a noise.
8. Do you want to go to a movie?
9. Do you want to watch TV?
10. Do you need a ride to the party?

B. Listen again to the sentences in Part A and repeat them.

C. Work with a partner. Take turns reading aloud the sentences in Part A. Be sure to group words together and to join the groups smoothly.

4 GAME: *Chain sentences*

A. Listen to these phrases and repeat them.

Noun	Place	Time
1. a. the books	b. to the library	c. at 1:30
2. a. my laundry	b. to the basement	c. on Monday
3. a. the packages	b. to the cleaners	c. at 7:00
4. a. the car	b. to the post office	c. tomorrow
5. a. your mother	b. to the mechanic	c. at 3:00
6. a. my homework	b. to the teacher	c. in the morning
7. a. the boxes	b. to the doctor	c. on Thursday

B. Work in groups of three. Make chain sentences.

Student 1: Start the sentence with "Please take" and a noun from Exercise A.

Student 2: Repeat Student 1's sentence and add a place from Exercise A.

Student 3: Repeat Student 2's sentence and add a time from Exercise A.

Then switch roles: Student 3 will start, Student 1 will add the place, and Student 2 will add the time.

EXAMPLE

Student 1: Please take the books . . .

Student 2: Please take the books to the library . . .

Student 3: Please take the books to the library on Monday.

---

5 SCRAMBLED MESSAGES

Make sure you understand the words in the box.

| plumbing | sink | pager | remind | dental hygienist |

A. Listen to the six messages on Professor Anderson's voice mail.

B. Work with a partner. Read the phrases in each column. Match phrases from each column to make six logical sentences describing Professor Anderson's messages.

A	B	C
1. Professor Anderson's computer	has a dentist appointment	from school today
2. The Education Committee	needs a ride	tomorrow morning
3. Professor Anderson's daughter	will meet	at the bookstore
4. Professor Anderson	has a meeting	until 7
5. The plumber	is waiting	from 3 to 4 tomorrow
6. Mrs. Anderson	can't fix the sink	until Monday

1. _____

2. _____

3. _____

4. _____

5. _____

6. _____

C. Practice reading the messages. Group words together. Join the groups together smoothly.

🎧 **First listen to:**

- the phrases in Exercise 1.
- the sentences in Exercise 2.

📼 **Now record them.**

Then write five sentences like the ones in Exercise 4. Record them.

Be sure to group words together and to speak smoothly.

Self-Study: See pages 169–170.

Joining final sounds to beginning sounds

INTRODUCTION

Final Consonant + Beginning Vowel

brown eyes   last October   ask Anna

- Join a final consonant to a beginning vowel clearly.
- A final consonant before a vowel is easy to hear.

Final Consonant + Different Beginning Consonant

book bag   start now   watch movies

- When the final consonant is [p], [b], [t], [d], [k], or [g], say it and hold it (⌐). Then say the next consonant.
- Don't separate the two consonants with a vowel sound.
- Keep the final consonant short.

Final Consonant + Same Beginning Consonant

finish shopping   one night   big girl

- When the same consonants come together, say one long consonant.
- When the same consonants are [p], [b], [t], [d], [k], or [g], hold that consonant.
- Don't say the consonant twice.

Final Vowel + Beginning Vowel

say it   play a game   How often?   show Andy

- When two vowels come together, use [y] or [w] to join them.
- Use [y] to join [ey], [ay], [iy], or [oy] to the next word.
- Use [w] to join [ow], [uw], or [aw] to the next word.

    y
see a movie [iy]   Who is it? [uw]   Go out. [ow]

- In words like *see*, the joining sound [y] is not written, but we say it.
- In words like *who* and *go*, the joining sound [w] is not written, but we say it.

FOCUSED PRACTICE

1 LISTEN AND PRACTICE: *Joining consonants to vowels*

A. Listen to these phrases and sentences and repeat them. Join the consonant and vowel clearly.

1. Clean up.
2. a big animal
3. the right answer
4. It's expensive.
5. Come in.

6. It's interesting.
7. the Pacific Ocean
8. That's OK.
9. his office
10. six o'clock

11. an old address
12. brown eyes
13. this evening
14. Leave early.
15. Jack ate it.

B. Choose four phrases and sentences from Part A and write them on the lines.

Your phrases: _____   _____

_____   _____

C. Work with a partner. Read your phrases to your partner. Your partner will write what you say. Then listen to your partner's phrases. Write them on the lines.

Partner's phrases: _____   _____

_____   _____

2 LISTEN AND PRACTICE: *Joining final consonants to different consonants*

A. Listen to these phrases and sentences and repeat them. Keep the final consonant short. Don't separate the consonants with a vowel sound.

1. Watch TV.
2. a large family
3. a white car
4. a big fish
5. hard questions

6. a good book
7. five children
8. a cold night
9. a wide sidewalk
10. dark glasses

11. a big dog
12. Which one?
13. a big city
14. I love pizza.
15. You look tired.

B. Choose four phrases and sentences from Part A and write them on the lines.

Your phrases: _____ _____

_____ _____

C. Work with a partner. Read your phrases to your partner. Your partner will write what you say. Then listen to your partner's phrases. Write them on the lines.

Partner's phrases: _____ _____

_____ _____

---

3 **LISTEN AND PRACTICE:** *Joining final consonants to the same consonant*

A. Listen to these phrases and sentences and repeat them. Don't say the consonant twice. Make one long consonant.

1. this student	6. a good dancer	11. Call Linda.
2. a black car	7. night time	12. a bad day
3. a quiet train	8. one number	13. Come Monday.
4. Stop playing.	9. Talk quietly.	14. this city
5. those zebras	10. five vans	15. a car radio

B. Choose four phrases and sentences from Part A and write them on the lines.

Your phrases: _____ _____

_____ _____

C. Work with a partner. Read your phrases to your partner. Your partner will write what you say. Then listen to your partner's phrases. Write them on the lines.

Partner's phrases: _____ _____

_____ _____

4 LISTEN AND PRACTICE: *Joining vowels*

A. Listen to these phrases and sentences and repeat them. Use [y] or [w] to join the vowels.

1. three apples [y]
2. How often?
3. I know it.
4. Do it. [w]
5. Say it.

6. two elephants [w]
7. Don't be angry. [y]
8. Go out. [w]
9. There's no answer. [w]
10. Play outside.

11. a new apartment
12. blue eyes [w]
13. Who is it? [w]
14. Monday afternoon
15. Try again.

B. Choose four phrases and sentences from Part A and write them on the lines.

Your phrases: _____ _____

_____ _____

C. Work with a partner. Read your phrases to your partner. Your partner will write what you say. Then listen to your partner's phrases. Write them on the lines.

Partner's phrases: _____ _____

_____ _____

5 LISTEN FOR DIFFERENCES: *Final and beginning sounds in compound nouns*

A. Look at the compound nouns below. Follow these directions:

If the underlined consonants are different, write *D*.
If the underlined consonants are the same, write *S*.
If the underlined sounds are a consonant and a vowel, write *CV*.

1. drugstore   _D_
2. bike path   ___
3. bull's-eye   ___

4. bus stop   ___
5. post office   ___
6. bookcase   ___

7. weekday ___   10. watch band ___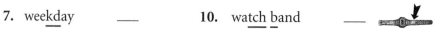

8. street address ___    11. zip code ___

9. ticket taker ___

B. Listen to the compound nouns in Part A and repeat them. Say the first noun on a high pitch.

C. Listen to these phrases and repeat them. Group words together.

1. Monday, Tuesday, Wednesday, Thursday, or Friday

2. someone who takes tickets

3. part of a watch

4. a place to buy medicine

5. a place to keep books

6. the middle of a target

7. a place to mail a letter

8. a path for bicycles

9. a five-digit number that follows the state name in an address

10. an address on a street

11. a place to catch a bus

D. Work with a partner. Take turns asking questions about the compound nouns in Part A and answering them with phrases from Part C. Be sure to join words together. Use this model:

Student 1: What's a drugstore?

Student 2: A drugstore's a place to buy medicine.

Work with a partner. Complete these dialogues, choosing compound nouns from Exercise 5. Then practice the dialogues. Join words together and speak clearly.

1. **Receptionist:** Dr. Benton is here Monday, Tuesday, and Thursday.

   Paulo: I can't come in on a _____. Doesn't he have any weekend hours?

2. **Sam:** When you go to the _____, pick up some toothpaste.

   Pete: I'm not going to the _____. I'm going to the grocery store.

3. **Sondra:** Where's my dictionary? I left it here on my desk.

   Lee: Look in the _____. I think I saw it there.

4. **Jin:** Why aren't you wearing your watch?

   Maria: My _____ broke. I need to get a new one.

5. **Lucy:** My mother really enjoyed meeting you last night.

   Lisa: I liked her, too. What's your _____ and _____? I want to send her a thank-you note.

6. **Young boy:** Can I go across the bridge on my bike?

   Police officer: Not on this side. The _____ is on the west side of the bridge.

🎧 **First listen to:**

- the phrases and sentences in Exercises 1–4.

▶️ **Now record them.**

Self-Study: See pages 170–171.

INTRODUCTION

Intonation can rise or fall after the strongest word in a sentence.

Did you READ it?

Last NIGHT.

Rising Intonation

Can you COME?

APPLES, BANANAS, GRAPES,...

- Intonation often rises on *yes/no* questions.
- Intonation rises on words in a list. It usually falls at the end of the list.
- Rising intonation can mean we aren't sure.
- Rising intonation can mean we aren't finished speaking.

Falling Intonation

I'm too TIRED to go.

TWO or THREE?

What do you MEAN?

- Intonation often falls after the strongest word in a sentence.
- Intonation often falls after the strongest word in *wh-* questions (questions with *Who, What, Where,* etc.).
- Intonation usually falls on the last word in a list.
- Falling intonation can mean we think what we're saying is correct.
- Falling intonation can mean we're finished speaking.

FOCUSED PRACTICE

A. Listen to these phrases and sentences, and repeat them. The strongest word is in capital letters. Follow the intonation lines.

1. Am I LATE?

2. Do you LIKE it?

3. WHEN? MONDAY? TUESDAY?

4. Are you READY?

5. on SUNDAY

6. It's RAINING.

7. She's from TEXAS.

8. It's on the TABLE.

9. APRIL or MAY?

10. RED, WHITE, and BLUE

11. NOW or LATER?

12. I want EGGS, JUICE, and COFFEE.

B. Choose three phrases and sentences from Part A and write them on the lines.

Your phrases:

_____ _____ _____

C. Work with a partner. Read your phrases to your partner. Your partner will write what you say. Then listen to your partner's phrases. Write them on the lines.

Partner's phrases:

_____ _____ _____

2 **DIALOGUES**

A. Listen to these dialogues and repeat them. Follow the intonation lines.

1. **Jose:** Do you want to GO?

   Ali: MAYBE.

2. **Marko:** I FOUND something.

   Susan: My KEYS?

3. **Lee:** She's from DALLAS.

   Maria: From DALLAS?

4. **Abdul:** Do you want MILK or CREAM?

   Lucy: MILK.

5. **Anna:** Are you going TODAY?

   Chang: TOMORROW.

6. **Carlo:** How much IS it?

   Clerk: Forty DOLLARS.

B. Work with a partner. Practice the dialogues in Part A.

---

3 LISTEN AND PRACTICE: *Recognizing different intonations*

A. Listen to these sentences and repeat them.

1. TWO, please. ⬎
2. SALAD. ___
3. A new DRESS? ___
4. SMITH. ___
5. 9:00 (NINE). ___
6. To the GYM. ___
7. Do you want to go OUT? ___

8. What's your LAST name? ___
9. ONE? ___
10. Do you want SOUP or SALAD? ___ ___
11. MAYBE. ___
12. At 9:30 (nine-THIRTY)? ___
13. I BOUGHT something. ___
14. Where are you GOING? ___

B. Listen to Part A again. Listen carefully to the intonation of the words in capital letters. Is the intonation rising or falling? Write intonation lines in the blanks (___⟋ or ⟍).

C. Work with a partner. Complete these dialogues with sentences from Part A. Mark the intonation. Then practice the dialogues.

1. **A:** I BOUGHT something.

   B: *A new DRESS?* _____

2. **A:** _____

   B: No, NINE.

3. **A:** _____

   B: To the GYM.

4. A: Do you want SOUP or SALAD?

   B: _____

5. A: _____

   B: SMITH.

6. A: Do you want to go OUT?

   B: _____

7. A: ONE?

   B: _____

4 DIALOGUE

A. Listen to the dialogue and repeat the lines. Follow the intonation lines.

Dan: How have you been? I haven't seen you for a while. How is Ivana?

Zoran: We broke up—about a month ago.

Dan: That's too bad—I guess. Is it too bad?

Zoran: Not really. We didn't have that much in common.

Dan: Are you seeing anyone else?

Zoran: No. But I'm thinking about asking Ivana's friend out. What do you think?

Dan: Her friend? I don't know about that. Do you think that's a good idea?

B. Practice the dialogue with a partner. Then answer this question:

Do you think Zoran should date his ex-girlfriend's friend? Why or why not?

ON YOUR OWN

First listen to:
- the phrases and sentences in Exercise 1.
- the dialogues in Exercise 2.

Now record them.

Self-Study: See pages 172–173.

UNIT 28 Using your voice to show your feelings

INTRODUCTION

Intonation and stress can show how you feel.

  Great.   Great.   Great.

- "Musical" intonation can show you're happy or interested.
- Low intonation and strong stress can mean you're upset or angry.
- Flat intonation can mean you're bored or tired or that you don't want to talk.

FOCUSED PRACTICE

I LISTEN AND PRACTICE: *Listening for feelings*

A. Listen to the conversations. Circle the word that describes how Lucy feels.

1. Joseph: Are you going to the party?
   Lucy: Yes.   (angry)   happy   bored

2. Joseph: I found your sweater.
   Lucy: Great.   angry   happy   bored

3. Joseph: I got an A on the test.
   Lucy: Great.   angry   happy   bored

4. Joseph: Do you want to see a movie?
   Lucy: OK.   angry   happy   bored

5. Joseph: Where's Bob?
   Lucy: At the beach.   angry   happy   bored

6. Joseph: Do you like my new haircut?
   Lucy: It's nice.   angry   happy   bored

B. Listen again to the conversations in Part A and repeat them.

C. Work with a partner. Practice each dialogue in Part A three times. The first time, say Lucy's part with an angry voice. The second time, say Lucy's part with a happy voice. The third time, say Lucy's part with a bored voice. Take turns reading Joseph's and Lucy's parts.

D. Work in groups. Follow these directions. Take turns until everyone in your group asks and answers a question.

Student 1:	Ask one of Joseph's questions in Part A. Choose a classmate to answer.
Student 2:	Say Lucy's part. Choose an angry voice, a happy voice, or a bored voice.
Other students:	Decide how "Lucy" feels.

2 LISTEN AND PRACTICE: *Recognizing different intonations*

A. First read the conversations. Ali can answer Max's question in two ways. Answer (a) means Max didn't hear what Ali said (or didn't hear everything). Answer (b) means Max heard what Ali said and wants more information.

1. **Ali:** I bought something.
    Max: What? _____
    Ali: **a.** I said I bought something.   **b.** A sweater.

2. **Ali:** There's a test tomorrow.
    Max: When? _____
    Ali: **a.** Tomorrow.   **b.** At 11:00.

3. **Ali:** There's a party at school tonight.
    Max: Where? _____
    Ali: **a.** At school.   **b.** In the gym.

4. **Ali:** I met a student today.
    Max: Who? _____
    Ali: **a.** I said I met a student.   **b.** Carlos Mendoza.

5. **Ali:** I'll call you tonight.
    Max: When? _____
    Ali: **a.** Tonight.   **b.** At 7:00.

6. **Ali:** I got a package today.

   Max: What? _____

   Ali: **a.** I said I got a package.   **b.** The books I ordered.

B. Listen to the first two lines of the conversations in Part A. When Max doesn't hear Ali's sentence, he asks the question with strong stress and rising intonation. When Max hears Ali's question and wants more information, he says the question with falling intonation. Draw intonation lines (⌣ ⌢) in the blanks after the questions.

C. Listen again to the first two lines of the conversations in Part A. Listen to Max's voice when he says the question word. How will Ali answer Max's question? Circle Ali's answer.

D. Now listen to the complete conversations in Part A. Check your answers.

E. Work with a partner. Practice the conversations in Part A. When you read Max's question, use your voice so your partner knows how to answer. Take turns reading Max's and Ali's parts.

---

3 **LISTEN AND PRACTICE:** *Using intonation to show your feelings*

A. Work with a partner. Look at the pictures. Practice the dialogues, using your voice to show how the people in the pictures feel.

1.

2.

3.

4.

5.

6.

 B. Now listen to the dialogues in Part A.

---

4 GAME: *What?*

Work with a partner. Practice using intonation to ask information questions.

Student 1: You have four sentences. Read one to your partner.

Student 2: Listen to your partner's sentence. Ask a one-word question, using *What?*, *Where?*, or *When?* Decide whether you want Student 1 to repeat the sentence or to give you more information. Use rising intonation on the question if you want a repetition. Use falling intonation if you want more information.

Student 1: Listen carefully to the intonation Student 2 uses. Repeat your sentence or answer the question. Then read another sentence. When you finish your sentences, switch roles with Student 2.

Student 1's sentences are on page 182. Student B's sentences are on page 184.

> **EXAMPLE**
>
> **Student 1:** Something great happened!
> **Student 2:** What?
> **Student 1:** The teacher canceled the test.
> **Student 1:** Something great happened!
> **Student 2:** What?
> **Student 1:** I said something great happened.

🎧 **First listen to:**

- the conversations in Exercises 1 and 2.

📼 **Now record them,** imitating the intonation you hear.

Then read these situations. Record the dialogues, following the directions after each situation. Use your voice to show how you feel.

1. Your mother calls you. You're very happy. You just got a great job and you want to tell her.

    Mom: How are you?

    You: Fine. I just got a job.

2. Your roommate comes in. You're really tired, and you don't want to talk. You just got a job, but you don't really want it.

    Roommate: What's up?

    You: Not much. I got that job.

3. Your roommate comes in. You're really angry because your roommate never helps clean the apartment.

    Roommate: How was your day?

    You: Great! I washed your dishes, took the garbage out, and cleaned up your mess.

Self-Study: See pages 173–174.

UNIT 2   [iy] <u>ea</u>t and [ɪ] <u>i</u>t

A. You will hear a pair of words. Listen carefully to the vowel sounds in the two words. Are the vowel sounds the same or different? Write *S* for *same* or *D* for *different*.

1. ___   2. ___   3. ___   4. ___   5. ___   6. ___

B. You will hear a sentence. Look at the sentence in your book. Listen carefully to the vowel sound. Do you hear [ɪ] or [iy]? Circle the word you hear.

EXAMPLE

On the recording, you hear: *Ginny works in a small office.*
In your book, you circle: (Ginny)/Jeannie works in a small office.

Listen. Circle the word you hear.

1. I like that **mitt/meat**.

2. She always **slips/sleeps** on the floor.

3. Those **hills/heels** are very high.

4. What a big **ship/sheep**!

Listen again and repeat the sentences.

UNIT 3   [æ] b<u>a</u>d and [ɛ] b<u>e</u>d

A. Listen to the recording and repeat the words. Write the words in the blanks.

	[æ] (**had**)	[ɛ] (**head**)
1. _black_		
2. _____		
3. _____		
4. _____		
5. _____		
6. _____		

Listen again. Do you hear [æ] or [ɛ]? Check the correct column.

B. You will hear a sentence. Look at the sentence in your book. Listen carefully to the vowel sound. Do you hear [æ] or [ɛ]? Circle the word you hear.

> **EXAMPLE**
>
> On the recording, you hear: *I like bread.*
> In your book, you circle: I like **Brad**/**bread.**

🎧 Listen. Circle the word you hear.

1. That's a nice **pan/pen**.

2. Alice is **tan/ten**.

3. He's **Dad/dead**.

4. Her name is **Callie/Kelly**.

🎧 Listen again and repeat the sentences.

UNIT 4 [ɑ] cop and [ə] cup

🎧 A. You will hear a pair of words. Listen carefully to the vowel sounds in the two words. Are the vowel sounds the same or different? Write *S* for *same* or *D* for *different*.

1. ___   2. ___   3. ___   4. ___   5. ___   6. ___

B. You will hear a sentence. Look at the sentence in your book. Listen carefully to the vowel sound. Do you hear [ɑ] or [ə]? Circle the word you hear.

> **EXAMPLE**
>
> On the recording, you hear: *Where's the new cup?*
> In your book, you circle: Where's the new **cop**/**cup**?

🎧 Listen. Circle the word you hear.

1. I see a yellow **dock/duck**.

2. That's a pretty **collar/color**.

3. Is that **Don/done**?

4. The **boss/bus** is coming.

🎧 Listen again and repeat the sentences.

Review of [ə], [æ], and [ɑ]

A. Listen to the recording and repeat the words. Write the words in the blanks.

	[ə] (cup)	[æ] (cap)	[ɑ] (cop)
1. _____bag_____			
2. _____			
3. _____			
4. _____			
5. _____			
6. _____			
7. _____			
8. _____			
9. _____			
10. _____			

Listen again. Do you hear [ə], [æ], or [ɑ]? Check the correct column.

B. You will hear a sentence. Look at the sentence in your book. Listen carefully to the vowel sound. Do you hear [ə], [æ], or [ɑ]? Circle the word you hear.

EXAMPLE

On the recording, you hear: *Where's the new cup?*
In your book, you circle: Where's the new **cop/cup**?

Listen. Circle the word you hear.

1. **Dan/Don** is my brother.

2. We **ran/run** every day.

3. Are you **Don/done**?

4. There's a **sack/sock** on the floor.

Listen again and repeat the sentences.

Vowels + r: [ɑr] c<u>ar</u>, [or] f<u>our</u>, and [ər] b<u>ir</u>d

A. You will hear a pair of words. Listen carefully to the vowel sounds in the two words. Are the vowel sounds the same or different? Write *S* for *same* or *D* for *different*.

1. ___   2. ___   3. ___   4. ___   5. ___   6. ___

B. Listen to the recording and repeat the words. Write the words in the blanks.

	[ɑr] **(car)**	[or] **(four)**	[ər] **(bird)**
1. ___*party*___			
2. _____			
3. _____			
4. _____			
5. _____			
6. _____			

Listen again. Do you hear [ɑr], [or], or [ər]? Check the correct column.

C. You will hear a sentence. Look at the sentence in your book. Listen carefully to the vowel sound in the incomplete word.

> **EXAMPLE**
>
> On the recording, you hear: *That's the new girl.*
> In your book, you write: That's the new g_*ir*_l.

Listen. Complete the words with *ar, or,* or *ir.*

1. Look at that st___ !

2. M___k is very sh___t.

3. Is it f___ ?

4. Your sh___t is d___ty.

Listen again and repeat the sentences.

A. Listen to the recording and repeat the words. Write the words in the blanks.

	[θ] (three)	[ð] (this)
1. _____father_____		
2. _____		
3. _____		
4. _____		
5. _____		
6. _____		

Listen again. Do you hear [θ] or [ð]? Check the correct column.

B. Look at the sentences. Complete them with the correct words.

1. Your grandmother and your __grandfather__ are your grandparents.

2. There are three children in my family: me, my sister, and my

   _____.

3. The day after Wednesday is _____.

4. Most people have 32 _____ in their mouths.

5. March is the _____ month of the year.

6. I don't like these jeans, but _____ over there are really nice.

7. The opposite of *north* is _____ .

8. There are _____ days in June.

Listen. Check your sentences. Correct them if necessary.

Listen again and repeat the sentences.

UNIT 9   [p] <u>p</u>en, [b] <u>b</u>oy, [f] <u>f</u>oot, [v] <u>v</u>ery, and [w] <u>w</u>et

A. You will hear a pair of words. Listen carefully to the consonant sounds in the two words. Are the words the same or different? Write *S* for *same* or *D* for *different*.

Listen. Are the words the same or different? Write *S* or *D*.

1. ___   3. ___   5. ___   7. ___   9. ___

2. ___   4. ___   6. ___   8. ___   10. ___

B. You will hear a sentence. Look at the sentence in your book. Listen carefully to the consonant sound.

> **EXAMPLE**
>
> On the recording, you hear: *That parrot is dangerous.*
> In your book, you circle: That **ferret**/(**parrot**)is dangerous.

Listen. Circle the word you hear.

1. It's really **boring/pouring**!

2. There's a **box/fox** on the front porch.

3. Can you spell **berry/very**?

4. Bring this to the **coffee/copy** machine.

5. Did you say **"vest"/"west"**?

Listen again and repeat the sentences.

UNIT 10   [s] <u>s</u>un, [z] <u>z</u>oo, [ʃ] <u>sh</u>oe, and [ʒ] televi<u>s</u>ion

A. Look at the words in the box. Think about the underlined letter or letters in each word. What sound does it have? Write the words in the correct columns on the next page.

A<u>s</u>ia	ea<u>s</u>y	poli<u>c</u>e	televi<u>s</u>ion
bu<u>s</u>	gara<u>g</u>e	ro<u>s</u>es	u<u>s</u>ually
bu<u>s</u>iness	hor<u>s</u>e	<u>s</u>pecial	va<u>c</u>ation
deci<u>s</u>ion	ma<u>ch</u>ine	<u>s</u>ugar	wa<u>s</u>

[s]	[z]	[ʃ]	[ʒ]
_____	_____	_____	_____
_____	_____	_____	_____
_____	_____	_____	_____
_____	_____	_____	_____

🎧 Listen to the words in the box. Check your answers. Correct them if necessary.

🎧 Listen again and repeat the words.

B. Look at the sentences. Complete them with words from Part A.

1. Don't leave your car on the street. Park it in the _____.

2. A: Do you take _____ in your coffee?

   B: I _____ use a little, but I'm on a _____ diet so I can't have any today.

3. Call the _____ ! There's a bad accident. A _____ hit a car on the corner.

4. A: _____ Reiko in class yesterday?

   B: No, she's on _____ . She went to _____ to visit her family.

5. It's very _____ to grow _____ in my garden.

6. A: I finally bought an answering _____ for my phone.

   B: And I made a big _____ , too. I got a new _____ . It has over 100 channels.

7. A: What kind of _____ does your family have?

   B: We have a _____ farm.

🎧 Listen. Check your sentences. Correct them if necessary.

🎧 Listen again and repeat the sentences.

[tʃ] <u>ch</u>air and [dʒ] <u>j</u>et; [dʒ] <u>j</u>et and [y] <u>y</u>et

A. You will hear a pair of words. Listen carefully to the consonant sounds in the two words. Are the words the same or different? Write *S* for *same* or *D* for *different*.

1. ___   2. ___   3. ___   4. ___   5. ___   6. ___

B. You will hear a sentence. Look at the sentence in your book. Listen carefully to the consonant sound.

EXAMPLE

> On the recording, you hear: *Can you cash this for me?*
> In your book, you circle: Can you (cash)/catch this for me?

Listen. Circle the word you hear.

1. Sal's going to **jail/Yale**.

2. The **chips/ships** are gone.

3. Why did you say **"Jess"/"yes"**?

4. **Jerry/Cherry** loves fish.

5. Can I have my **chair/share** now?

6. Bob **chokes/jokes** a lot.

Listen again and repeat the sentences.

[r] <u>r</u>oad and [l] <u>l</u>ove

A. You will hear a pair of words. Listen carefully to the consonant sounds in the two words. Are the words the same or different? Write *S* for *same* or *D* for *different*.

1. ___   3. ___   5. ___   7. ___   9. ___

2. ___   4. ___   6. ___   8. ___   10. ___

B. You will hear a sentence. Look at the sentence in your book. Listen carefully to the consonant sound. Circle the word you hear.

EXAMPLE

> On the recording, you hear: *This is so light!*
> In your book, you circle: This is so (light)/right!

🎧 Listen. Circle the word you hear.

1. Do you want to meet a **pilot/pirate**?

2. The teacher **collects/corrects** our homework every day.

3. Why is this so **long/wrong**?

4. That **glass/grass** is beautiful.

5. They **play/pray** here every day.

🎧 Listen again and repeat the sentences.

UNIT 13   [m] <u>m</u>outh, [n] <u>n</u>ose, and [ŋ] si<u>ng</u>

🎧 A. Listen to the recording and repeat the words. Write the words in the blanks.

	[m] (mouth)	[n] (nose)
1. _____make_____		
2. _____		
3. _____		
4. _____		
5. _____		
6. _____		

	[ŋ] (sing)	[ŋg] (longer)
7. _____		
8. _____		
9. _____		
10. _____		
11. _____		
12. _____		

🎧 Listen again. In 1–6 do you hear [m] or [n]? In 7–12 do you hear [ŋ] or [ŋg]? Check the correct column.

B. You will hear a sentence. Look at the sentence in your book. Listen carefully to the consonant sounds in the incomplete words. Write *m, n,* or *ng.*

> **EXAMPLE**
>
> On the recording, you hear: *Bri___ Be___.*
> In your book, you write: Bri*ng* Be *n* .

🎧 Listen. Complete the words with *m, n,* or *ng.*

1. ___att is too th___ because he's never hu___ry.

2. ___oel is you___er than I a___ .

3. Ri___ the bell please, Jo___ .

4. Mr. Cha___ , this is Mr. Ki___ .

🎧 Listen again and repeat the sentences.

C. You will hear a sentence. Look at the sentence in your book. Listen carefully to the consonant sound. Do you hear [m], [n], or [ŋ]? Circle the word you hear.

> **EXAMPLE**
>
> On the recording, you hear: *That's neat!*
> In your book, you circle: That's **meat/(neat)**!

🎧 Listen. Circle the word you hear.

1. You're **Ron/wrong**!

2. How do you spell *win/wing*?

3. Has it **run/rung** today?

4. There are a lot of **teams/teens** here.

🎧 Listen again and repeat the sentences.

Word endings: plurals and present tense

🎧 A. Listen to the recording and repeat the words. Write the words in the blanks.

	[əz]/[ɪz] (roses)	[z] (dogs)	[s] (starts)
1. _____oranges_____			
2. _____			
3. _____			
4. _____			
5. _____			
6. _____			

🎧 Listen again. Is the s ending pronounced [əz]/[ɪz], [z], or [s]? Check the correct column.

B. Look at the underlined words in the sentences. Think about the s ending in each word. What sound does it have? Write the correct sound above each word: [əz]/[ɪz], [z], or [s].

             [əz]
1. Bill won two <u>prizes</u> at the party.

        [ ]   [ ]   [ ]
2. The <u>students</u> learn many <u>things</u> in their <u>classes</u>.

              [ ]   [ ]
3. You need several <u>pencils</u> for the <u>tests</u>.

        [ ]   [ ]   [ ]
4. Anna <u>leaves</u> work at 4:30 and <u>goes</u> to her <u>parents</u>' house.

          [ ]   [ ]   [ ]
5. My brother <u>walks</u> to school on <u>Mondays</u> and <u>Wednesdays</u>.

          [ ]   [ ]
6. Our father <u>drives</u> him to school on <u>Tuesdays</u>.

       [ ]   [ ]
7. He <u>takes</u> the bus on <u>Fridays</u>.

      [ ]   [ ]
8. Who <u>washes</u> the <u>dishes</u> after dinner?

🎧 Listen. Check your answers. Correct them if necessary.

🎧 Listen again and repeat the sentences.

A. Look at the verbs in the box. Think about the past tense ending of each verb. Is it pronounced [əd], [t], or [d]? Write the past forms in the correct columns.

called	decided	invited	ordered	studied
cleaned	ended	laughed	stayed	wanted
cooked	hated	liked	stopped	watched

[əd] / [ɪd] (**visited**)	[t] (**helped**)	[d] (**arrived**)
_____	_____	_____ *called* _____
_____	_____	_____
_____	_____	_____
_____	_____	_____
_____	_____	_____

🎧 Listen to the verbs. Check your answers. Correct them if necessary.

🎧 Listen again and repeat the verbs.

B. Complete the conversation with past tense forms from Part A.

A: What did you do last night? Did you go out?

B: No, I _____ home. I _____ dinner and _____ the kitchen. Then I _____ TV and _____ some friends on the phone. Oh, and I _____ for my English test. How about you?

A: I _____ to see the new James Bond movie, so I _____ Marie to go with me.

B: How was the movie? Did you like it?

A: I _____ it, but Marie didn't. In fact, she _____ it.

B: Did you do anything after the movie?

A: It _____ pretty late, but we _____ we were hungry.

We _____ at Rosie's Diner on our way home. We

_____ cake and coffee—and we _____ a lot. Marie

is very funny!

🎧 Listen. Check your answers. Correct them if necessary.

🎧 Listen again and repeat the conversation.

UNIT 16 Consonant groups

🎧 **A. You will hear a pair of words. Listen carefully to the consonant sounds in the two words. Are the words the same or different? Write _S_ for _same_ or _D_ for _different_.**

1. ___   2. ___   3. ___   4. ___   5. ___   6. ___

🎧 Listen again and repeat the words.

B. Look at the phrases. What words do they describe? Write the correct words.

1. a word that means _mad_ _____*angry*_____

2. the opposite of _noisy_ _____

3. a color that rhymes with _too_ _____

4. the season before summer _____

5. the number after eleven _____

6. the place students go to study _____

7. what we do when we're very sad _____

8. the opposite of _work_ _____

9. what January and February are _____

10. the opposite of _quickly_ _____

🎧 Listen. Check your answers. Correct them if necessary.

🎧 Listen again and repeat the words and phrases.

Strong stress and secondary stress in words

A. Listen to the recording and repeat the words. Write the words in the blanks.

	First syllable	Middle syllable	Last syllable
1. _____elephant_____			
2. _____			
3. _____			
4. _____			
5. _____			
6. _____			
7. _____			
8. _____			
9. _____			
10. _____			

Listen again. Is the strong stress on the first syllable, the middle syllable, or the last syllable? Check the correct column.

B. Look at the short conversations. Which words and syllables have strong stress? Mark them with an accent mark (′).

1. A: What do you want for dinner?

   B: How about pasta and a salad?

2. A: Do you like bananas?

   B: Yes, I love them. They're delicious.

3. A: How do you feel today?

   B: I feel pretty good. I slept really well last night.

4. A: How's your new apartment?

   B: It's terrible. My neighbors are noisy, and my refrigerator doesn't work.

🎧   Listen. Check your answers. Correct them if necessary.

🎧   Listen again and repeat the conversations.

UNIT 19   Weak syllables in words

A. Look at the words. Which syllables are stressed? Which aren't? Circle the weak syllables in the words.

1. din (ner)
2. A las ka
3. A pril
4. gui tar
5. bro ken
6. Au gust

🎧   Listen. Check your answers. Correct them if necessary.

🎧   Listen again and repeat the words.

B. Look at the sentences. Think about the weak syllables and strong syllables. Circle the vowels in the bold words that are pronounced [ə].

1. Go (a)**way**!
2. The **police** are here.
3. This is **Alaska**.
4. I'm leaving in **April**.
5. He's **famous**.
6. Who'll be here **tonight**?
7. Don't **open** that now!
8. It's six **o'clock**.

🎧   Listen. Check your answers. Correct them if necessary.

🎧   Listen again and repeat the sentences.

UNIT 20 Stress in compound nouns and numbers

A. Match the nouns in column A with the correct nouns in column B. Then write the compound nouns. Which word in each compound noun has strong stress and high pitch? Mark the stressed word with an accent mark (′).

A	B	
1. tennis	a. office	1. _ténnis court_
2. frying	b. store	2. _____
3. bus	c. card	3. _____
4. running	d. court	4. _____
5. office	e. stop	5. _____
6. post	f. room	6. _____
7. park	g. pan	7. _____
8. birthday	h. bench	8. _____
9. grocery	i. building	9. _____
10. living	j. shoes	10. _____

Listen. Check your answers. Correct them if necessary.

Listen again and repeat the words.

B. You will hear a sentence. Look at the sentence in your book. Listen carefully to the pronunciation of the number. Circle the number you hear.

EXAMPLE

On the recording, you hear: *He's 13.*
In your book, you circle: He's (13)/30.

Listen. Circle the number you hear.

1. About **15/50** people came to the party.
2. That dress is **$79.99/$799.99**.
3. This birthday card is **$2.19/$2.90**.
4. Is your address **3015/3050** Oak Street?
5. When did they move to **17th/70th** Street?
6. The post office is at **414/440** Main Street.

Listen again and repeat the sentences.

A. Listen to the conversation. Write the weak words in the blanks.

Fran: Rob! Hi! How _____are_____ you?

Rob: Great! How _____ you?

Fran: _____ great. _____ so glad _____ see
_____ .

Rob: Same here. What's new?

Fran: _____ having _____ party. _____ _____
Friday.

Rob: That sounds _____ fun. What time?

Fran: _____ _____ eight. _____ _____
Halloween party.

Rob: Should _____ wear _____ costume?

Fran: Absolutely.

Rob: OK, Fran. _____ see _____ next Friday _____
eight. Thanks _____ _____ invitation.

Fran: _____ welcome. See _____ then.

🎧 Listen. Check your answers. Correct them if necessary.

🎧 Listen again and repeat the conversation.

B. Mr. Smith's secretary took a message for him while he was out for lunch.
   Read the information.

His wife called from City Hospital. His sister, Mary, had a baby boy.
The baby weighs seven pounds and is healthy. He should call his wife
at 555-2186.

What did Mr. Smith's secretary tell him when he got back from lunch?
Complete the message.

Please _____ your _____. She's at _____

_____. Your _____, _____, had a

_____ _____. He weighs _____ pounds and is

_____. The phone number is _____.

🎧 Listen and check your answers. Correct them if necessary.

🎧 Listen again and repeat the message.

UNIT 22 | Highlighting the strongest word

A. You will hear a sentence. Listen carefully for the highlighted word. Underline the highlighted word.

> **EXAMPLE**
>
> On the recording, you hear: *Charlene went out with TOM last night.*
> In your book, you underline: Charlene went out with Tom last night.

🎧 Listen to the sentence. You will hear it five times. Each time the highlighted word will be different. Underline the highlighted word.

1. John bought a new red Jaguar on Monday.

2. John bought a new red Jaguar on Monday.

3. John bought a new red Jaguar on Monday.

4. John bought a new red Jaguar on Monday.

5. John bought a new red Jaguar on Monday.

🎧 Listen again and repeat the sentence. Highlight the correct word each time.

B. Look at the conversations. The **bold** word in A's information is incorrect. B replies with the correct information. Write B's replies. Then underline the highlighted word in the corrected information.

1. A: Grass is **blue**.

   B: *No, grass isn't blue. It's green.*

2. A: English pronunciation is **easy**.

   B: _____

3. A: The sky is **green**.

    B: _____

4. A: The day after Saturday is **Monday**.

    B: _____

🎧   Listen and check your answers. Correct them if necessary.

🎧   Listen again and repeat the conversations.

UNIT 23   Common weak words

🎧   **A.** Listen to the phrases. Does the speaker say _and_ or _or_? Write _and_ or _or_ in the blank.

    1. right _____ wrong

    2. black _____ white

    3. off _____ on

    4. June _____ July

    5. chocolate _____ vanilla

    6. play the piano _____ sing

🎧   Listen again and repeat the phrases.

🎧   **B.** You will hear Alex's friend Susan talk about things he can and can't do. Listen to the sentences and circle _can_ or _can't._

    1. Alex can/can't play soccer well.

    2. He can/can't speak English very well.

    3. He can/can't understand a lot.

    4. He can/can't understand American movies.

    5. He can/can't drive.

C. You will hear a question. Listen carefully to the pitch. Does the question ask about two choices? If you hear choices, mark the two pitches. (There are three questions that are not about choices.)

> **EXAMPLE**
>
> On the recording, you hear: *Do you want meat or fish?*
> In your book, you mark the pitch:
>
> Do you want meat or fish?

Listen to the choice questions. Mark the two pitches.

1. Do you want salt or pepper?

2. Are you married or single?

3. Does he want coffee or tea?

4. Is she going to cook or clean up?

5. Do they want one or two?

6. Is May or June better for you?

Listen again and repeat the sentences.

UNIT 24 Contractions

A. You will hear a sentence. Look at the sentence in your book. Listen carefully. Do you hear a contraction or the full form of the verb? Circle the word or phrase you hear.

> **EXAMPLE**
>
> On the recording, you hear: *That is terrible!*
> In your book, you circle: **That's/That is** terrible!

Listen. Circle the word or phrase you hear.

1. The **teacher's not/teacher is not** here today.

2. I **didn't/did not** like that movie.

3. You **aren't/are not** eating your dinner.

4. I think **it's/it is** raining.

5. We **can't/cannot** go out tonight.

6. He **doesn't/does not** work very hard.

7. **They'd/They would** like to see you.

8. **I'll/I will** see you there.

Listen again and repeat the sentences.

B. You will hear a sentence. Look at the sentence in your book. Listen carefully to the contraction. Write the contraction you hear.

1. _____I'm_____ not married.

2. We _____ come tonight.

3. _____ time for class.

4. _____ late!

5. _____ call you tomorrow.

6. _____ going to miss the show.

7. _____ never liked that actress.

8. _____ 25.

Listen again and repeat the sentences.

UNIT 25 | Word groups

A. Look at the sentences. Think about word groups. Mark possible word groups for each sentence. (There is more than one way to group the words in most sentences.)

1. I need to buy a new computer.

2. Let's watch a movie on TV tonight.

3. Don't do your homework in the kitchen.

4. We go to the beach every Sunday afternoon.

5. Why did you put your books on the floor?

6. Dan's plane lands at 5:30 tomorrow evening.

7. Give the teacher your homework.

8. The children are playing in the street.

🎧 Listen and repeat the sentences. Are your word groups the same as the ones on the recording? (Remember: There is more than one way to group the words in most sentences.)

B. **Read the conversation. Think about word groups and which words have strongest stress.**

A: There's a test on Wednesday.

B: Oh, no! Not Wednesday! I'm going to a party Tuesday night. I have to go. It's my sister's birthday party.

A: You can study before the party.

B: I can't. I promised to take Sue to dinner first.

A: Who's Sue?

B: She's this great girl I met last week. We met in the library.

A: Well, you have a problem.

B: I know. What can I do?

A: Sorry, pal. I really don't know.

🎧 Listen to the conversation. Mark the word groups.

🎧 Listen again. In each sentence, circle the word (or words) with strongest stress.

🎧 Listen again and repeat the conversation.

UNIT 26 Joining final sounds to beginning sounds

A. Look at the sentences on the next page. Think about how the final sound of the first word is joined to the beginning sound of the second word. Which pattern does it follow? Write the letter of the pattern—A, B, C, or D—next to each sentence. Then mark the joining: ‿ or *y* or *w*.

> **A.** consonant + vowel: Find Eli.
> **B.** consonant + different consonant: Speak softly.
> **C.** consonant + same consonant: Walk quickly.
> **D.** vowel + vowel: See a movie.

1. Stop it. <u>A</u>

2. Good dog! ___

3. Hurry up. ___

4. It's snowing. ___

5. It's cold. ___

6. Walk faster. ___

7. Speak English. ___

8. It's seven-thirty. ___

9. Go away. ___

10. Play outside. ___

🎧 Listen and check your answers. Correct them if necessary.

🎧 Listen again and repeat the sentences.

B. Look at the sentences. Think about how the final and the beginning vowel sounds are joined. Are they joined with *y* or with *w*? Write the correct sound between the final vowel and the beginning vowel in each sentence.

1. Don't go ^wout today.

2. She's coming Tuesday afternoon.

3. She wants to be a dancer.

4. Who is it?

5. He has blue eyes.

6. They'll be over later.

7. This zoo has three elephants.

8. I called, but there was no answer.

🎧 Listen and check your answers. Correct them if necessary.

🎧 Listen again and repeat the sentences.

UNIT 27 Rising and falling intonation

A. **Listen to the sentences and questions. Do they end with rising intonation or falling intonation? Check the correct column.**

	⌣	⌢
1. How much salad do you want?		
2. Are you going out?		
3. Why do you look so angry?		
4. Let's get some cheese.		
5. We could get some cookies, too.		
6. Your intonation is great!		
7. Does Jake ever sit down?		
8. I'd like to try the new Italian restaurant.		

Listen again and repeat the sentences.

B. **Look at the conversation. Think about the intonation at the end of each sentence. Mark the intonation. Draw intonation lines (⌣ or ⌢) at the end of each sentence.**

Dan: Hi, Lee. I need your help. Can you help me?

Lee: Sure, Dan. What's the problem?

Dan: This class. I'm terrible at math.

Lee: When do you want to study?

Dan: This afternoon?

Lee: This afternoon? Ok. What time?

Dan: At four?

Lee: Fine. In the dorm?

Dan: Is the library ok?

Lee: Of course. See you then.

🎧 Listen. Check your answers. Correct them if necessary.

🎧 Listen again and repeat the conversation.

UNIT 28 Using your voice to show your feelings

A. Read the four conversations between Mary and her husband, Jack.

🎧 Listen to the conversations. How does Jack feel? angry, happy, or bored? Check the correct column.

1. **Mary:** Hey, Jack! Amy called.
   Jack: Great. Just great.   angry   happy   bored

2. **Mary:** Did you hear the news, Jack? John has a new girlfriend.
   Jack: Wonderful.   angry   happy   bored

3. **Mary:** Oh, Jack. I forgot to tell you. Fred and Sally invited us to a party. I said yes.
   Jack: Terrific.   angry   happy   bored

4. **Mary:** Let's go to the movies tonight.
   Jack: Good idea.   angry   happy   bored

🎧 Listen again and repeat the conversations.

B. Look at the first two lines of the conversations. Sometimes B's question means "I didn't hear what you said." Sometimes it means "I heard you, and I want more information." Think about the intonation for each kind of question and A's possible reply.

1. **A:** I'm planning a trip next spring.
   B: When?
   A: a. I said next spring.   **b.** In June.

2. **A:** I saw an old friend today.
   B: Who?
   A: **a.** I said an old friend.   **b.** My college roommate, Lila.

3. **A:** I really want to go to college.
   B: Where?
   A: **a.** I said to college.   **b.** Probably a state university.

4. **A:** Paul gave me a beautiful gift.
   B: What?
   A: **a.** I said Paul gave me a beautiful gift.   **b.** A silver bracelet.

5. **A:** I want something to eat.
   B: What?
   A: **a.** I'm hungry. I need to eat.   **b.** Maybe a sandwich.

Listen carefully to the first two lines of the conversations. Think about how A will reply. Circle the correct answer.

Listen to the complete conversations and check your answers. Correct them if necessary.

Listen again and repeat the conversations.

SELF-STUDY ANSWER KEY

UNIT 2

Part A, p. 149
1. D feel–fill   2. S it   3. D live–leave
4. D these–this   5. S seat   6. D rich–reach

Part B, p. 149
1. mitt   2. sleeps   3. heels   4. ship

UNIT 3

Part A, p. 149
1. [æ] black   2. [ɛ] then   3. [æ] man   4. [ɛ] west
5. [ɛ] pen   6. [æ] ask

Part B, p. 150
1. pan   2. ten   3. dead   4. Callie

UNIT 4

Part A, p. 150
1. D shot–shut   2. S some   3. S not
4. D cluck–clock   5. D once–wants
6. D cot–cut

Part B, p. 150
1. dock   2. color   3. Don   4. bus

UNIT 5

Part A, p. 151
1. [æ] bag   2. [ɑ] cop   3. [ə] run   4. [ə] month
5. [ə] nut   6. [æ] Dan   7. [ɑ] Ron   8. [æ] ran
9. [ɑ] bog   10. [æ] stand

Part B, p. 151
1. Don   2. run   3. done   4. sack

UNIT 6

Part A, p. 152
1. S hard   2. D were–war   3. D for–far
4. S heart   5. D burn–barn   6. D shirt–short

Part B, p. 152
1. [ɑr] party   2. [or] morning   3. [ər] learn
4. [or] warm   5. [ər] first   6. [ɑr] Mark

Part C, p. 152
1. star   2. Mark, short   3. far   4. shirt, dirty

UNIT 8

Part A, p. 153
1. [ð] father   2. [θ] thick   3. [θ] tooth
4. [ð] this   5. [θ] bath   6. [ð] breathe

Part B, p. 153
1. grandfather   2. brother   3. Thursday   4. teeth
5. third   6. those   7. south   8. thirty

UNIT 9

Part A, p. 154
1. S fox   2. D west–vest   3. S very   4. S pear
5. D copy–coffee   6. D bear–pear
7. D berry–very   8. D vote–boat
9. D ferret–parrot   10. D robe–rope

Part B, p. 154
1. pouring   2. box   3. very   4. coffee   5. west

UNIT 10

Part A, p. 154

[s]: bus   decision   horse   police

[z]: business   easy   roses   was

[ʃ]: machine   special   sugar   vacation

[ʒ]: Asia   garage   television   usually

Part B, p. 155

1. garage   2. sugar, usually, special   3. police, bus   4. Was, vacation, Asia   5. easy, roses
6. machine, decision, television
7. business, horse

UNIT 11

Part A, p. 156

1. D sheep–cheap   2. D wash–watch   3. S ship
4. D catch–cash   5. D mush–much   6. S chair

Part B, p. 156

1. Yale   2. chips   3. Jess   4. Cherry
5. share   6. jokes

UNIT 12

Part A, p. 156

1. S lock   2. D right–light   3. D alive–arrive
4. D led–red   5. S wrong   6. D redder–letter
7. D fry–fly   8. D lace–race   9. S pilot
10. S long

Part B, p. 156

1. pilot   2. corrects   3. wrong   4. glass   5. play

UNIT 13

Part A, p. 157

1. [m] Make   2. [n] dinner   3. [n] nine   4. [n] know   5. [n] Nat   6. [m] Moe   7. [ŋ] ringer
8. [ŋ] young   9. [ŋg] finger   10. [ŋ] wrong
11. [ŋ] wing   12. [ŋg] longer

Part B, p. 158

1. Matt, thin, hungry   2. Noel, younger, am
3. Ring, Jon   4. Chang, Kim

Part C, p. 158

1. wrong   2. wing   3. run   4. teams

UNIT 14

Part A, p. 159

1. [əz] oranges   2. [əz] watches   3. [s] sleeps
4. [s] students   5. [z] leaves   6. [z] does

Part B, p. 159

1. [əz]   2. [s], [z], [əz]   3. [z], [s]
4. [z], [z], [s]   5. [s], [z], [z]   6. [z], [z]
7. [s], [z]   8. [əz], [əz]

UNIT 15

Part A, p. 160

[əd]: decided; ended; hated; invited; wanted

[t]: cooked; laughed; liked; stopped; watched

[d]: called; cleaned; ordered; stayed; studied

Part B, p. 160

A: What did you do last night? Did you go out?
B: No, I **stayed** home. I **cooked** dinner and **cleaned** the kitchen. Then I **watched** TV and **called** some friends on the phone. Oh, and I **studied** for my English test. How about you?
A: I **wanted** to see the new James Bond movie, so I **invited** Marie to go with me.
B: How was the movie? Did you like it?
A: I **liked** it a lot, but Marie didn't. In fact, she **hated** it.
B: Did you do anything after the movie?
A: It **ended** pretty late, but we **decided** we were hungry. We **stopped** at Rosie's Diner on our way home. We **ordered** cake and coffee—and we **laughed** a lot. Marie is very funny!

UNIT 16

Part A, p. 161
1. D thing–think   2. D start–star   3. S shirt
4. D clothes–closes   5. D month–months
6. S built

Part B, p. 161
1. *angry*   2. *quiet*   3. *blue*   4. spring   5. twelve
6. school   7. cry   8. play   9. months
10. *slowly*

UNIT 18

Part A, p. 162
1. elephant (First syllable)   2. vacation (Middle syllable)   3. Australia (Middle syllable)
4. university (Middle syllable)   5. begin (Last syllable)   6. o'clock (Last syllable)   7. ocean (First syllable)   8. July (Last syllable)
9. Mexico (First syllable)   10. potatoes (Middle syllable)

Part B, p. 162
1. **A:** Whát do you wánt for dínner?
   B: How about pásta and a sálad?
2. **A:** Do you líke banánas?
   B: Yés, I lóve them. They're delícious.
3. **A:** Hów do you feél todáy?
   B: I feél pretty goód. I slépt reálly well last níght.
4. **A:** Hów's your new apártment?
   B: It's térrible. My neíghbors are noísy, and my refrígerator doesn't wórk.

UNIT 19

Part A, p. 163
1. din(ner)   2. (Alaska)   3. A(pril)   4.(guitar)
5. brok(en)   6. Au(gust)

Part B, p. 163
1. Go@way!   2. The p(o)lice are here.   3. This is Alask@   4. I'm leaving in A(pril)   5. He's fa(mous)
6. Who'll be here(to)night?   7. Don't o(pen) that now!   8. It's six (o)clock.

UNIT 20

Part A, p. 164
1. ténnis court   2. frýing pan   3. bús stop
4. rúnning shoes   5. óffice building
6. póst office   7. párk bench   8. bírthday card
9. grócery store   10. líving room

Part B, p. 164
1. About **15** people came to the party.
2. That dress is **$799.99**.
3. This birthday card is **$2.19**.
4. Is your address **3050** Oak Street?
5. When did they move to **17th** Street?
6. The post office is at **440** Main Street.

UNIT 21

Part A, p. 165
Fran: Rob! Hi! How **are** you?
 Rob: Great! How **are** you?
Fran: **I'm** great. **I'm** so glad **to** see **you**.
 Rob: Same here. What's new?
Fran: **I'm** having **a** party. **It's on** Friday.
 Rob: That sounds **like** fun. What time?
Fran: **It's at** eight. **It's a** Halloween party.
 Rob: Should **I** wear a costume?
Fran: Absolutely.
 Rob: OK, Fran. **I'll** see **you** next Friday **at** eight. Thanks **for the** invitation.
Fran: **You're** welcome. See **you** then.

Part B, p. 165

Please **call** your **wife**. She's at **City Hospital**. Your **sister, Mary**, had a **baby boy**. He weighs **seven pounds** and is healthy. The phone number is **555-2186**.

UNIT 22

Part A, p. 166

1. Jaguar   2. John   3. Monday   4. red   5. new

Part B, p. 166

1. A: Grass is **blue**.
   B: No, grass isn't **blue**. It's **green**.
2. A: English pronunciation is **easy**.
   B: No, English pronunciation isn't **easy**. It's **hard**.
3. A: The sky is **green**.
   B: No, the sky isn't **green**. It's **blue**.
4. A: The day after Saturday is **Monday**.
   B: No, the day after Saturday isn't **Monday**. It's **Sunday**.

UNIT 23

Part A, p. 167

1. and   2. and   3. or   4. or   5. and   6. or

Part B, p. 167

1. can   2. can't   3. can   4. can   5. can't

Part C, p. 168

1. Do you want salt or pepper?
2. Are you married or single?
3. Does he want coffee or tea?
4. Is she going to cook or clean up?
5. Do they want one or two?
6. Is May or June better for you?

UNIT 24

Part A, p. 168

1. teacher's not   2. did not   3. aren't   4. it's
5. cannot   6. doesn't   7. They would   8. I'll

Part B, p. 169

1. I'm   2. can't   3. It's   4. He's   5. We'll
6. They're   7. He's   8. We're

UNIT 25

Part A, p. 169

1. I need to buy a new computer.

2. Let's watch a movie on TV tonight.

3. Don't do your homework in the kitchen.

4. We go to the beach every Sunday afternoon.

5. Why did you put your books on the floor?

6. Dan's plane lands at 5:30 tomorrow evening.

7. Give the teacher your homework.

8. The children are playing in the street.

Part B, p. 170

A: There's a test on Wednesday.

B: Oh, no! Not Wednesday! I'm going to a party Tuesday night. I have to go. It's my sister's birthday party.

A: You can study before the party.

B: I can't. I promised to take Sue to dinner first.

A: Who's Sue?

B: She's this great girl I met last week. We met in the library.

A: Well, you have a problem.

B: I know. What can I do?

A: Sorry, pal, I really don't know.

UNIT 26

Part A, p. 170

1. A   2. C   3. D   4. C   5. B   6. B   7. A   8. B
9. D   10. D

Part B, p. 171

1. Don't go out today.

2. It's on Tuesday afternoon.

3. She wants to be an artist.

4. Who is it?

5. He has blue eyes.

6. They'll be over later.

7. This zoo has three elephants.

8. I called, but there was no answer.

UNIT 27

Part A, p. 172

1. \
2. /
3. \
4. \
5. \
6. \
7. /
8. \

Part B, p. 172

Dan: Hi, Lee. I need your help. Can you help me?

Lee: Sure, Dan. What's the problem?

Dan: This class. I'm terrible at math.

Lee: When do you want to study?

Dan: This afternoon?

Lee: This afternoon? OK. What time?

Dan: At four?

Lee: Fine. In the dorm?

Dan: Is the library ok?

Lee: Of course. See you then.

UNIT 28

Part A, p. 173
1. angry   2. bored   3. happy   4. bored

Part B, p. 173
1. b   2. a   3. a   4. b   5. a

UNIT EXERCISE ANSWERS

UNIT 8

Exercise 4
Part B, page 39
1. d 2. e 3. c 4. f 5. a 6. g 7. j 8. h 9. b
10. i

Part C, pages 39–40
1. Christmas
2. Halloween
3. New Year's Eve
4. April Fool's Day
5. Memorial Day
6. New Year's Day
7. Valentine's Day
8. Independence Day
9. Thanksgiving
10. Labor Day

UNIT 17

Exercise 3
Part B, page 91
Cities: Boston, Dallas, Atlanta
States: Texas, Wisconsin, Florida, Michigan
Countries: China, Jamaica, Korea, Canada,
  Portugal

UNIT 22

Exercise 4
Part B, pages 118–119
1. There are **60** minutes in an hour.
2. There are **30** days in September. *or* There are
   31 days in **January** (and in March, May, July,
   August, October, and December).
3. Miami is in **Florida.** *or* **Dallas** is in Texas.
4. The President of the United States lives in the
   White House.

5. Water freezes at **0°** (zero degrees) Centigrade.
6. Chicago is a **big** city.
7. Mexico is **south** of the United States. *or*
   Canada is north of the United States. *or*
   Mexico is north of **Guatemala.**
8. April is the **fourth** month of the year. *or*
   March is the third month of the year.
9. A square has **four** corners. *or* A **pentagon**
   has five corners.
10. A red traffic light means "**Stop.**" *or* A **green**
    traffic light means "Go."
11. Boston is a city in the **United States.** *or*
    Montréal is a city in Canada.
12. There are **24** hours in a day.
13. The Titanic was a large **ship.**
14. Shakespeare was a famous **English** writer. *or*
    Lady Murasaki was a famous Japanese writer.

UNIT 23

Exercise 1
Part D, page 121
1. rice and beans
2. bacon and eggs
3. bread and water
4. surf and turf
5. cookies and milk
6. cake and ice cream
7. chips and dip
8. turkey and stuffing
9. salt and pepper
10. fish and chips

APPENDIX I: for team I players

UNIT 6

Exercise 6, page 31
1. What's the third month of the year?
2. What do you find in a dictionary?
3. What does a man wear under a jacket?
4. What's the opposite of *last?*
5. What's the past tense of *are?*
6. What's the opposite of *clean?*
7. What's the opposite of *finish?*
8. What's the opposite of *remember?*
9. What number comes after 32?

Answers:
1. March   2. words   3. (a) shirt   4. first
5. were   6. dirty   7. start   8. forget
9. 33

UNIT 8

Exercise 3, page 38
1. What's the opposite of *north?*
2. What day comes after Wednesday?
3. What's the name of the white things in your mouth?
4. What do you say when someone does something nice?
5. What street comes between Fourth Street and Sixth Street?
6. What number comes after 29?
7. What's a word for things you wear?
8. What can you do with a ball?
9. What's the plural of *that?*
10. What's the opposite of *everything?*

Answers:
1. south   2. Thursday   3. teeth
4. Thanks / Thank you   5. Fifth (Street)   6. 30
7. clothing   8. throw (it)   9. those   10. nothing

UNIT 9

Exercise 6, page 46
1. What letter comes after *U?*
2. What is the opposite of *morning?*
3. What do many people drink in the morning?
4. What's the opposite of *noisy?*
5. What's another word for *persons?*
6. What's the opposite of *white?*
7. What's another word for *a male child?*
8. What's the opposite of *east?*
9. What number comes after 6?
10. What's the opposite of *slow?*
11. What month comes after January?

Answers:
1. V   2. evening   3. coffee   4. quiet   5. people
6. black   7. boy   8. west   9. 7   10. fast/quick
11. February

UNIT 20

Exercise 2B, page 108

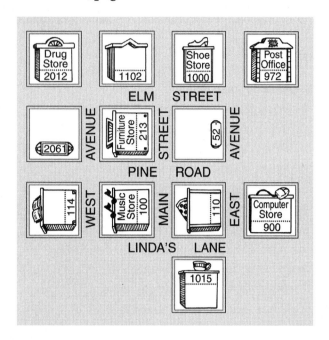

Ask your partner about the address on your map with blanks.

What's at *1102 Main Street*?

Your partner will tell you the answer. Write the answer in the blank.

UNIT 28

Exercise 4, page 147

1. Something terrible happened.
2. I'll meet you this afternoon.
3. Let's go to the country.
4. There's something on your shirt.

APPENDIX II: for team 2 players

UNIT 6

Exercise 6, page 31
1. What's a Ford?
2. What's the name of a round shape?
3. What's the opposite of *south*?
4. What do people do at their jobs?
5. What animals fly?
6. What's the opposite of *after*?
7. What number comes after 3?
8. What's the opposite of *easy*?
9. What number comes after 29?

Answers:
1. (a) car   **2.** (a) circle   **3.** north   **4.** work
5. birds   **6.** before   **7.** 4   **8.** hard   **9.** 30

UNIT 8

Exercise 3, page 38
1. What's the name for the day you were born?
2. What's the opposite of *south*?
3. What number comes after 999 (nine hundred ninety-nine)?
4. What part of your face is under your nose?
5. What's a word for your mother's son?
6. What's the plural of *this*?
7. Where do you go to see a movie?
8. What's the opposite of *healthy*?
9. What's 1 + 2?
10. What is January?

Answers:
1. birthday   **2.** north   **3.** (one/a) thousand
4. mouth   **5.** brother   **6.** these
7. (a) theater   **8.** unhealthy
9. 3   **10.** (a) month (the first month)

UNIT 9

Exercise 6, page 46
1. What season is between fall and spring?
2. What's the opposite of *an answer*?
3. What do people speak?
4. What's a word for *a male parent*?
5. What's the opposite of *start*?
6. What do we call the front of the head?
7. What's the opposite of *unhappy*?
8. What number comes after 4?
9. What's the opposite of *always*?
10. What's the opposite of *after*?
11. What's the opposite of *small*?

Answers:
1. winter   **2.** a question   **3.** language(s)
4. father (papa, pop, pa)   **5.** finish/stop
6. face   **7.** happy   **8.** 5   **9.** never   **10.** before
11. big

UNIT 20

Exercise 2B, page 108

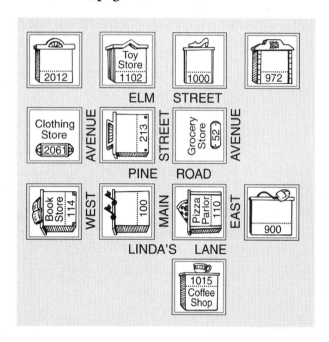

Ask your partner about the address on your map with blanks.

What's at *2012 Elm Street*?

Your partner will tell you the answer. Write the answer in the blank.

UNIT 28

Exercise 4, page 147

1. Something strange happened.

2. I have some good news.

3. Let's get together this weekend.

4. I met Felix on campus.